Market Opportunity Analysis

Market Opportunity Analysis

Robert E. Stevens
Northeast Louisiana University

Philip K. Sherwood
Winona Research

Lexington Books
D.C. Heath and Company/Lexington, Massachusetts/Toronto

Library of Congress Cataloging-in-Publication Data

Stevens, Robert E., 1942–
    Market opportunity analysis.

    Includes bibliograpies and index.
    1. Marketing research. 2. Market surveys. I. Sherwood, Philip K. II. Title.
HF5415.2.S775   1986   658.8'3   86-10548
ISBN 0-669-13228-4 (alk. paper)

Published simultaneously in Canada
Printed in the United States of America
International Standard Book Number: 0-669-13228-4
Library of Congress Catalog Card Number

The paper used in this publication meets the minimum requirements of American National Standard for Information Sciences—Permanence of Paper for Printed Library Materials, ANSI Z39.48-1984.
∞™

86 87 88 89 90 8 7 6 5 4 3 2 1

This book is dedicated to all the market analysts and marketing practitioners who have helped forge the way for increasing the effectiveness and efficiency of our country's marketing efforts.

Contents

List of Figures   xi

List of Tables   xiii

Preface and Acknowledgments   xvii

I   Introduction to Market Opportunity Analysis   1

1. **Market Opportunity Analysis: An Overview   3**

   The Importance of Market Opportunity Analysis   3
   Why Strategic Planning?   3
   Strategic Planning: Key to Success   4
   What Is Strategy?   5
   Factors Influencing Market Opportunity Analysis   5
   What Is Market Opportunity Analysis?   8
   Plan of the Book   9

2. **Strategic Management and Planning   11**

   Resistance to Strategic Planning   11
   The Strategic Management Process   12
   Corporate Purpose or Mission   14
   Corporate Objectives   16
   Identifying Market Opportunities   19
   Strategies for Existing SBUs   22
   Summary   24

II   External Analysis   25

3. **Market Demand Analysis   27**

   Identifying a Market   27
   Market Factors   31
   Summary   37

4. **Competitive Analysis 39**

Purpose of Competitive Analysis 39
Types of Competition 40
Level of Competition 41
Deciding on the Nature of the Competition 41
Competitive Advantages 42
Industry Analysis 43
Competitor Analysis 46
The Competitive Market Mix Audit 47
Competitive Strategies and Resources 49
Search for a Differential Advantage 51
Positioning the Company/Product 51
Summary 52

III **Financial Analysis 55**

5. **Revenue and Cost Analysis 57**

Nonprofit Financial Analysis 58
Forecasting Market Share 59
Cost Analysis 61
Cost Concepts 61
Types of Costs 62
Data Sources 65
Cost Behavior, Sensitivity Analysis, and Risk Analysis 66
Summary 77

6. **Profitability Analysis 79**

Return on Investment 79
Financial Analysis 80
Methods of Analyzing Investments 82
Summary 93

IV **Internal Analysis 95**

7. **Internal Analysis 97**

Problems versus Opportunities 97
Internal Factors 98
Ranking Opportunities 101
Summary 103

Appendixes 105

Appendix A. Sources of Data for Market Opportunity Analysis 107

Appendix B.   Sample Market Opportunity Analysis Reports   115
Index   179
About the Authors   187

List of Figures

1–1. Market Opportunity Analysis   9

2–1. The Strategic Planning Process   13

2–2. Product/Market Growth Matrix   20

2–3. Boston Consulting Group Business Portfolio Matrix   22

3–1. Grid 1 for Shoes   29

3–2. Grid 2 for Shoes   30

4–1. Competitive Forces   46

5–1. Break-Even   68

5–2. Scatter Diagram   76

List of Tables

3–1. Consumer Characteristics by Consumer Type   31

3–2. Soft Contact Lens: Sales Index Method   33

3–3. The Market Factor Method   34

3–4. Estimating Market Potential Using Multiple Regression Analysis   35

3–5. Market Potential for an Ironing Board Attachment in the Southeastern United States   36

4–1. Effects of Competitive Environment   42

4–2. Industry Evaluation Factors   45

4–3. Competitive Market Mix Audit Form   48

4–4. Comparative Pricing: Restaurants   50

5–1. Pro Forma Income Statement   58

5–2. Attendance Projections   60

5–3. Cost Categories   69

5–4. Sensitivity Analysis of Production and Profits   70

5–5. Sensitivity Analysis of Price and Profits   70

5–6. Cost Forecast Checklist   71

5–7. Project Cost Summary   75

6–1. Calculation of Payback Period   83

6–2. Net Present Values for Two Alternative Projects   86

6–3. Present-Value Index   89

6–4. Expected Values for Cash Flow Calculations without Adjustment for Risk   90

6–5. Expected Values for Cash Flow Calculations with Adjustment for Risk   91

6–6. Cost/Benefit Ratio Analysis   92

7–1. Company Resource Evaluation Matrix   101

7–2. Analysis of Strengths and Weaknesses   102

7–3. Summary of Opportunity Analysis Worksheet   103

B–1. Overall Market Characteristics   128

B–2. Pro Forma Income Statements   132

B–3. Estimated Market Area Beef Consumption for 1985   140

B–4. Estimated Market Area Pork Consumption for 1985   141

B–5. Inventory of Cattle and Hogs in State 1, State 2, and State 3, 1985   142

B–6. Consumption, Slaughter, and Imports of Beef and Pork in State 1, State 2, and State 3, 1985   143

B–7. Breakdown of Building Costs   144

B–8. Other Building Costs   145

B–9. Summary of Facility Costs   147

B–10. Sales Revenues by Product Type   148

B–11. Cost of Animal Inputs   149

B–12. Salary Schedule for Administrative and Office Personnel   150

B–13. Total Annual Employee Expense Schedule   151

B–14. Debt Retirements and Interest Schedule   152

B–15. Pro Forma Income Statement   153

B–16. Rollco Packing Company: Breakdown of Building Cost Estimates   154

B–17. Overnight Visitors to Northwest Madison, 1986   159

B–18. Camping Activity in Madison, 1982–1986   160

B–19. Camper Party Nights: State and Region   161

B–20. Northwest Madison Population and Income Statistics 161

B–21. RV Trailer Parks by Type of Amenities 162

B–22. RV Park Cost Estimates 169

B–23. Proposed Recreational-Vehicle Park Projected Income Statement by Park Size and Occupancy Level 170

B–24. Sixty-Space Recreational-Vehicle Park Pro Forma Income Projections 172

B–25. Return on Investment Calculations 173

Preface and Acknowledgments

The 1980s have been called the decade of planning in a recent American Marketing Association publication. The book, *Market Opportunity Analysis*, presents a systematic approach to market analysis that is philosophically sound and practically oriented. The philosophical base is the strategic management orientation, which is quickly becoming the main approach to the marketing process. The practical orientation is achieved through the emphasis on techniques and tools used in preparing a market opportunity analysis. A step-by-step approach carries the reader through the market opportunity analysis process. The emphasis throughout is on (1) what needs to be done and (2) how to do it.

There were two main reasons for writing this book. The first was that one of the most common types of decisions business people make is whether or not to enter a new market or to market a new product. An extensive market opportunity analysis is a prerequisite to such decisions. Thus this book addresses a topic in which most business people are involved—one that produces significant "bottom line" results.

The second reason grew out of the first. Since we were unable to find such a book, we began to develop our own approaches and to put together a systematic format for conducting a market opportunity analysis. Over the past twenty years, we have conducted numerous studies involving market opportunity analysis and this book contains the basic approaches we have developed, plus what we have learned from others writing in the same area.

A book is seldom the work of the authors alone, and this one is no exception. Many people helped us get this manuscript in final form. We would especially like to thank Jane Olsen for typing and coordinating many aspects of the work; Jeaneen Kunick and Robert Roller for helping proofread and update material; and John Blaho who provided input into one of the studies in the appendix, as did Dr. Tom Ivy and Dr. Carle Hunt. Special thanks are also due to Elaine Drain and Marcella Rodgers for typing the manuscript through its many revisions.

Part I
Introduction to Market Opportunity Analysis

1
Market Opportunity Analysis: An Overview

The Importance of Market Opportunity Analysis

The 1980s have ushered in an era for business that is one of the most challenging in history. Markets for many products have weakened; major firms face crucial financial crises (The Dow Jones Industrial average of thirty industrial stocks is now the Dow Jones twenty-nine, with the Manville Corporation, in bankruptcy); international competition for major product categories is at an all-time high; financial markets are in an upheaval as a result of interest-rate changes and uncertainty over future rates; and shifting government policies on tax decreases, increases, and deficit spending are only some of the most obvious environmental factors with which business managers must cope.

Although these changes have created havoc in many industries, they have also caused many managers to reevaluate the basis of success in their own industry and in business more generally. Many have realized that the key to success is *planning*—not just short-range planning but long-run (or strategic planning) as well.

This book concentrates on market opportunity analysis, an intricate part of the strategic planning process. It not only covers how opportunity analysis relates to strategic planning, but also presents the techniques that can be used to carry out an opportunity analysis. Thus it is oriented toward building individual managers' analytical skills by describing what they should do and how.

Why Strategic Planning?

Out of the large number of decisions made by an organization's managers, there are a handful of crucial ones that have a significant impact on the future of that organization or individual. The same is true for products and services. Strategic decisions require identification and thoughtful consideration. In the past several decades, many major U.S. corporations have focused on short-term improvements in market position and profitability. Meanwhile, the Japanese have made great strides because of their willingness to sacrifice short-term profitability for market share.

Perspectives on strategic thinking can be illustrated with this question: Who are the two most important individuals responsible for the success of an airplane's flight? Frequent responses are the pilot and the navigator, or the pilot and the maintenance supervisor, or the pilot and the air traffic controller, or the pilot and the flight engineer. All these responses recognize the day-to-day hands-on importance of the pilot, and they all introduce some other important support or auxiliary functionary to the answer. Each of these responses, however, ignores the person who is perhaps the single most important individual in determining the ultimate success of the airplane—the designer. The pilot and the designer may well be the two most important individuals in this respect—the pilot because of the day-to-day responsibilities involved in commanding the craft, and the designer because of the ability to create a concept that can be economically constructed, easily operated by any normally competent flight crew, and maintained safely by the ground crew.

Most modern executives perceive themselves as pilots of their organization: taking off, landing, conferring with the navigator, communicating with the air traffic controller. They generally view themselves as the chief hands-on operational manager. However, what has been most lacking in U.S. industry in the past few years has been an appreciation for the long-run strategic viewpoint. There is a need for more emphasis on the "designer" approach to operating an organization. A well-conceived strategic planning system can facilitate this emphasis.

Strategic Planning: Key to Success

Many of the large business combinations of the 1920s did not survive into the 1950s. Some economists have predicted that between now and the 1990s we can expect to see many of our large corporate institutions faltering. There is trouble in Detroit and difficulty with some large equipment manufacturers and some financial institutions. This trend is likely to continue. Many of our current institutions have developed excessive overhead costs—a negative development. Strategic planning development must not lead to a larger and larger number of people creating more and more reports for other people to read. It cannot become a peripheral activity that has little direct impact on the actual making of goods and services. Rather, strategic planning can be consistent with decreasing overhead and increasing productivity. In fact, many consider the lack of a strategic orientation the biggest problem facing industry today. In order to compete successfully, a company must strategically eliminate the high-overhead structure that is characteristic of the end of an economic long wave.

Planning is one of the keys to success of any undertaking, and nowhere is it more important than in business. Every study dealing with business failures uncovers the same basic problem, whether it is called undercapitalization, poor location, or simply a lack of managerial skills. All these problems are rooted in poor planning. Strategic planning of operations from a market perspective can become a key to the long-term survival and growth of an organization.

What Is Strategy?

Before discussing the market opportunity analysis process in more detail, it is important to establish clear-cut definitions of the terms *strategic* and *strategy*. This will provide a better perspective on market opportunity analysis, which is an integral part of the process of strategy development.

The word *strategic* means "pertaining to strategy" and is derived from the Greek word meaning "generalship," "art of the general," or more broadly "leadership." The word *strategic*, when used in the context of planning, provides a perspective on planning that is long run in nature and deals with achieving specified end results. Just as military strategy has as its objective winning the war, so too strategic planning has as its objective achieving corporate objectives—survival and growth.

Strategic decisions must be differentiated from tactical ones. Strategic decisions outline the overall game plan or approach, whereas tactical decisions involve implementing the various activities needed to carry out a strategy.

Marlboro cigarettes, a product of Philip Morris, Inc., was positioned years ago as a cigarette aimed at the male smoking market. This was a strategic decision made by Phillip Morris's executives for this specific product. Given this strategy, many tactical decisions were made about the color and size of wording on the package, the atmosphere in which the product was consumed in advertising, the image portrayed by the people used in the ads, and so forth. These were tactical decisions that were needed to implement the strategic decisions previously made. Thus the strategic decision provides the overall framework within which the tactical decisions are made. It is crucial that managers be able to differentiate between these types of decisions to identify whether the decision has short- or long-term implications.

Strategy development is a process of (1) identifying strategic options and opportunities, (2) analyzing or defining these options and opportunities, and (3) selecting the opportunities to pursue and specifying how they will be pursued.

Factors Influencing Market Opportunity Analysis

The strategic opportunities of an enterprise are influenced by factors of three types: external factors, financial considerations, and internal factors. External factors include market size, competitive technology, the economy, government, political conditions, social change, and nature.

External Considerations

Market Size. The size and makeup of markets for goods and services influence the nature of the opportunities an organization faces. The growth and longevity of markets influence not only whether opportunities will be pursued but also the level of commitment a firm will make to pursue an opportunity.

Competition. Some companies and some markets focus strategic planning around the current or anticipated behavior of their competitors. Some managers emphasize that corporate strategy must revolve around competitors' behavior.

Technology. Major technological advances tend to create opportunities for companies prepared to capitalize on them. The computer chip, the electronic transistor, and synthetic fiber have all led to minor revolutions in their respective markets.

Inflation and the Economy. After several decades of stable prices, inflation became a definite factor for planners in the 1970s. A nation's basic economic conditions will determine the range of opportunities available to organizations. Inflation, tight money, high interest rates, and cash flow problems are all part of the economic circumstances that confront firms today and necessitate appropriate strategic planning. Even the largest and most powerful corporations have not been immune to these problems. For example, General Motors has had its bond rating lowered because of changing economic and financial considerations.

Government Regulations. The role of government in the regulation of economic life has increased in all major industrial nations. Government influences many phases of marketing, including distribution, advertising, price policy, product design, and consumer use. Although government regulations present both restraints and opportunities, their side effects have often been higher costs. Pollution control devices, reporting requirements, tax policy (for example, windfall taxes), safety policy, and other government controls and regulations have added costs to the industry and the consumer. Evaluation of existing and proposed legislation is an essential part of strategic planning for all organizations.

Political Conditions. The introduction of political risk should be an essential part of any organization's strategic planning. The oil crisis of 1974 and general political instability have altered the state of the art of planning within many companies dependent on unstable supplies of raw materials. An unavoidable part of today's international business environment is the uncertainty surrounding political events. The violent overthrow of the Pahlavi dynasty in Iran; the continuing conflict in Northern Ireland; some fifteen to twenty wars, border clashes, and guerrilla conflicts in Africa; and many similar events have increased anxiety over the role of political risk in overseas investment. No wonder strategic planners frequently use the word *turbulent* to describe the environment in which today's multinational companies must operate.

Social Change. Social change presents opportunities as well as hazards for business enterprises. Although these influences change only slowly over time, they can ultimately have a profound impact on the economic viability of a company. Social change can also have a drastic effect on the behavior of important groups of consumers. For example, technological innovation must be assimilated by consumers in order to become economically viable. For example, although the technology exists for a checkless economic environment, society has been slow to embrace it. The same may be true of what is sometimes called the office of the future or the paperless office. MKT's extensive research shows that although, again, the technology exists, there is great uncertainty regarding the social acceptance of this type of office. Major research efforts are constantly tracking social changes and attempting to evaluate their impact on business. Since many important social changes come slowly, businesses often fail to identify the significance of these changes for their activities until it is too late either to mitigate the damage or to capitalize on the opportunity.

Nature. Droughts and floods, blizzards and lack of snow—all have important impacts on business. Acts of nature are unpredictable, and these capricious environmental factors require proper planning.

Financial Considerations

Financial considerations reflect the financial impact of opportunities in terms of revenues, costs, and return on investment. They must reflect both the size of the investment needed to compete effectively in a market and the potential returns associated with that investment.

Revenue Estimates. Revenue estimates provide the essential data needed to assess the impact of market entry by a new competitor. A firm that is considering entering an existing market must assess its chances of attaining a given market share and thereby a specific stream of revenues. Estimates of sales revenues, along with cost estimates, provide the essential data for analysis of an opportunity.

Cost Estimates. Cost estimates reflect the level of costs that will be associated with the revenues generated by a proposed venture. It is extremely important that all costs be estimated to reflect accurately the income or cash flows that an opportunity will produce.

Return on Investment. Given the estimates of future revenues and costs, the next step in financial analysis is the analysis of return on investment. Here there are two concerns: (1) the level of investment needed to compete effectively and (2) the profitability potentials available given the investment level. In other words, "How much money will it take to pursue an opportunity?" and "What type of earnings can be produced?"

Internal Considerations

Internal factors include: (1) organizational purpose, (2) corporate objectives, and (3) resources.

Purpose. A statement of purpose or mission is management's expression of the nature of an organization. It attempts to answer two questions: "What kind of organization are we?" and "What kind of organization do we want to be?" The definition of purpose or mission becomes the guiding force in strategic decisions because what we do should be a function of what we are.

Corporate Objectives. Whereas a mission statement proposes to answer the question of what we are, a statement of corporate objectives answers the question "What do we want to accomplish?" Objectives become the specific ways a firm accomplishes its organizational mission, as well as the standard by which organizational effectiveness can be judged.

Resources. An organization's resources are the factors that allow a firm to accomplish objectives. Resources include the people, money, machinery, facilities, and so forth that a company either possesses or has the ability to acquire. An organization's base of people and material assets represents its capability to pursue opportunities.

Thus *external factors* define the nature of the opportunity, *financial considerations* tell us the financial impact of the opportunity, and *internal factors* determine whether a firm should pursue an opportunity (mission and objectives) and whether it is capable (resources) of pursuing an opportunity.

What Is Market Opportunity Analysis?

Market opportunity analysis is the process of defining the exact nature of the opportunities available in an organization's operating environment in terms of external, financial, and internal considerations. Figure 1–1 presents an overview

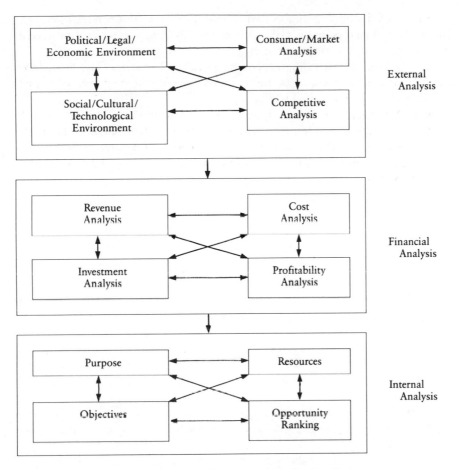

Figure 1–1. Market Opportunity Analysis

of this process in terms of the steps involved in the analysis. As the diagram depicts, market opportunity analysis is a comprehensive analysis of all aspects of an opportunity, performed before decisions are made to pursue the opportunity. The results of such an analysis give the decision maker a strong data base from which to choose the various opportunities present in the environment in line with the financial and internal considerations specified by management.

Plan of the Book

Chapter 2 presents the foundation for market opportunity analysis—strategic planning. This chapter provides the framework from which market opportunity analysis can be viewed as an integral part of the strategic management process.

Part II of the book contains two chapters dealing with external analysis. Environmental factors, market size and growth, and competitive analysis receive detailed treatment in these chapters.

Part III contains two chapters covering financial analysis. The procedures used to estimate revenues, costs, and return on investment are presented to provide complete coverage of this vital area.

Part IV presents internal analysis. It contains the material that moves from analysis to decision making as internal factors are evaluated in light of the market opportunities being considered. This material synthesizes all the analysis in a form that summarizes the analysis in one worksheet as a basis for pursuing opportunities.

2
Strategic Management and Planning

Many of today's most successful companies evolved out of an era in which they introduced a good product or service into a market that was ready to accept the product. Growth was achieved by expanding to new geographical markets and, later, by adding new products to build a complete line rather than concentrating on a single product. In many companies growth appeared to happen with little or no formal thought about the management processes that were leading to the growth.

With significant shifts in economic, environmental, and competitive forces, however, most managers have now realized that, if survival and growth are to occur, they must be much more aware of the impact of the decisions they are making and the management processes used to make these decisions. A switch to strategic planning is replacing the more intuitive decision-making approaches used in the past. For most companies, the key to success is strategic planning—and the key to strategic planning rests on matching market needs to corporate capabilities: *strategic fit.*[1]

Resistance to Strategic Planning

Although there is much academic and theoretical support for strategic planning, its actual implementation often runs aground on the shores of corporate reality. Even in high-tech companies there is significant resistance to strategic planning. Some of the most common arguments against strategic planning are:

1. Planning is not action oriented.
2. Planning takes too much time; we're too busy to plan.
3. Planning is unrealistic because of the rapid change in our industry (technological uncertainty and so forth).
4. Planning soon becomes an end in itself, not just a means to an end.

Many of these arguments stem from the kind of thinking that would conclude that the pilot plays the most important role in the success of an airplane. To be extremely helpful, strategic planning does not depend on complete forecasting accuracy. In fact, a variety of futuristic alternatives or scenarios can be very helpful in establishing strategic planning parameters. Often a best-case, most-likely case, and worst-case approach is used, as will be discussed later. This three-level forecast gives dimension to the process of recognizing, anticipating, and managing change.

The feeling that strategic planning is not a hands-on approach or is unrelated to the important day-to-day operations of the company is a common one in U.S. industry. This point of view, however, is shortsighted in terms of long-term success and profitability. Strategic planning is not just for dreamers; on the contrary, it lets the management team determine what can be done today to attain—or avoid—some future circumstance.

Strategic planning sometimes becomes an end in itself in the minds of some of its practitioners. This is particularly true when it is established solely as a staff responsibility within an organization. A support staff can facilitate the strategic planning process, but the process will not be a dynamic, vital activity of the organization without the ongoing involvement of top management and line managers. President Eisenhower has been widely quoted as saying, "Plans are nothing, planning is everything." The truth he expressed was that the plan itself was not the goal, but the process of planning—developing futuristic scenarios, evaluating the environment and the competition, assessing internal strengths and capabilities, revising objectives and tactics—was the organizational dialogue that was most important. This organizational dialogue ideally breaks down barriers to communication, exposes blind spots, tests logic, measures the environment, and determines feasibility. The result is more effective and efficient implementation of organizational activity.

The Strategic Management Process

Strategic management, whether at a corporate level involving whole companies or divisions or at an individual level involving a single product or service, is basically a matching process. This matching process involves analyzing opportunities in the marketplace as a market develops and then matching company resources to opportunities. The objective of this process is to peer through the "strategic window"[2] and identify opportunities that exist in the market of which the individual company is able to take advantage. Thus the *strategic management process can be defined as a managerial process that involves matching organizational capabilities to market opportunities.* These opportunities are created as a market evolves over time and decisions revolve around investing or divesting resources in these markets. The context in which these strategic decisions are made is: (1) the organization's operating environment, (2) company purpose or mission, and (3) objectives. This overall process is depicted in figure 2–1. Market opportunity analysis is the process that ties all these elements together to facilitate strategic choices that are consistent with all three areas.

A prerequisite to effective strategic planning is identifying the unit or level for which planning is to be done. Many companies have embraced a concept that is extremely useful in this strategic planning process—the *strategic business unit.*

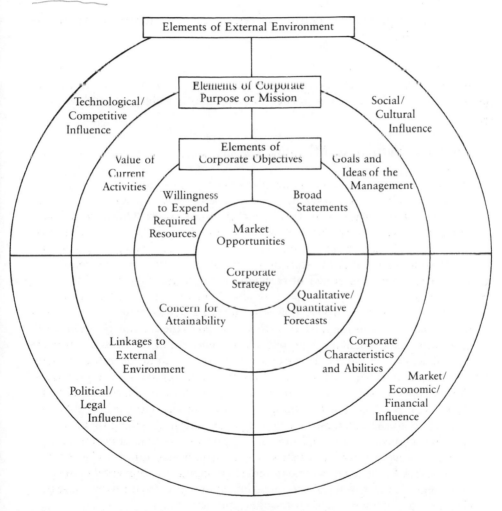

Figure 2–1. The Strategic Planning Process

A strategic business unit (SBU) meets the following criteria:

1. It serves a clearly defined served market or markets.
2. It is a full-fledged competitor in an external market, as opposed to being an internal supplier. As such it has at least one identifiable competitor.
3. It is a discrete unit—separate, distinct, and identifiable. It is possible to conduct integrated strategic planning related to markets, products, organizations, and facilities. Its assets do not depend on the existence of another SBU.
4. Its manager has full control over crucial decisions related to the success of the business.[3]

Once an organization's SBUs have been identified, strategic planning can be carried out for each SBU. However, care must be exercised to ensure that the activities of each SBU are related to corporate-level objectives and purpose.

Corporate Purpose or Mission

Drucker has referred to an organization's purpose as its mission or reason for being.[4] To define a business's purpose is to ask, "What is our business and, more important, what should it be?" Drucker further states: "Only a clear definition of the mission and purpose of the business makes possible clear and realistic business objectives. It is the foundation for priorities, strategies, plans, and work assignments. It is the starting point for the design of managerial jobs and above all for the design of managerial structure."[5]

One aspect of every firm's purpose should be to meet a need in the market place. A statement of purpose, however, must be a written statement that spells out in some detail the unique factors that have led to the creation of the business enterprise. Such a statement becomes a reference point for subsequent managerial action—in effect, the reference point on which all operating areas in a firm must reflect as a part of their decision-making processes. A typical question faced by most firms is whether to enter a particular market or introduce a particular product. The first thing to consider in answering is how this decision relates to the stated purpose of the organization. Anything that does not help the organization accomplish its stated purpose should not be undertaken, no matter how profitable or otherwise successful it may appear to be. A firm's purpose can be altered over time to reflect changing environmental conditions or changing managerial philosophies, but at any given point there must be a reference point for managerial thought and action.

A clear understanding of company purpose is needed to ensure alignment of activities with the way the firm has defined its mission. Otherwise, attempted activities may be at cross-purposes with the organizational mission, or, on the other hand, there may be a failure to attempt activities beneficial to fulfillment of that mission. *Common vision and unity can be achieved only by common purpose.*

The following statement of purpose, prepared by Colowyo Coal Company's management, is exemplary of the type of statement that can be developed to provide unity and guidance in decision making:

> The primary purpose of Colowyo Coal Company is to operate at a profit for the benefit of its owners, employees, and the community. Colowyo will produce its coal resources at optimum rates that will provide orderly community growth, protect the environment and contribute to alleviating our nation's energy needs.
>
> The Company is committed to adhering to its approved mining plan by following all laws, rules and applications with a minimum disturbance to the environment and timely restoration to disturbed areas.
>
> Our purpose is to produce a quality product and to provide superior services to its customers. Colowyo will provide a work environment for its employees that allows them, through training and other means, to achieve personal growth while helping the Company to achieve its stated objectives.
>
> An equal opportunity employer, Colowyo makes every effort to provide safe, healthful working conditions for its employees as it seeks to operate within the tenets of the free enterprise system.
>
> Finally, Colowyo is committed to conducting its business relationships in such a manner as to be a credit to its partners, employees and their families, customers and the community. The Company is proud to be a leader in the mining industry of our country.[6]

A few of the implications of this statement for market opportunity analysis will help show how to relate purpose to opportunity assessment. The first paragraph, for example, states that the company will produce at an optimum rate that provides orderly community growth, protects the environment, and so on. This means that Colowyo's strategies must not be based on an expansion of sales volume, which would cause a large increase in productive capacity and would involve both rapid community growth and less environmentally sound production techniques.

Another restraint can be derived from the third paragraph—"quality product." This stipulation limits market activities aimed at lower product quality to reach more cost-oriented customers or customers who actually want a lower-quality product.

These examples illustrate the impact of statements of purpose on opportunity analysis. Market activities must be consistent with overall purpose for an effective organization.

Corporate Objectives

Corporate objectives vary so widely in their nature and their content that it is difficult to describe in general terms what such objectives should be. Even the terms used to describe objectives vary widely: *policy, goals, values*, and *objectives* are often used interchangeably even within the same company. The definition used here is a generally accepted view of what is meant by objectives.

Basically, an objective is a desired end result. It is a statement of what is to be accomplished by an organization. It is tied to purpose in that achieving its objectives is the way the organization fulfills its purpose.

There are three objectives basic to any organization:

1. To engage in a business activity that is both economically and socially useful.
2. To maintain and/or survive as a business entity.
3. To grow in size of operations—whether measured by increases in sales, profits, number of employees, or some other criterion for growth.

These objectives are almost inherent to a business, although many firms do not formally state them. However, to provide more specific guidance to the organization, both as a statement of desired end results and as a tool for evaluating performance, objectives need to be more explicit in defining what is to be accomplished.

Peter Drucker has pointed out the importance of objectives that are more than abstractions in the following statement: "If objectives are only good intentions they are worthless. They must degenerate into work. And work is always specific, always has—or should have—unambiguous measurable results, a deadline and a specific assignment of accountability."[7]

The following section provides some examples of corporate objectives taken from statements of objectives of three corporations. Notice the differences in the degree of specificity of the objectives. Some companies state their objectives in a more quantifiable form; others do not. Quantified objectives can be evaluated on an absolute quantitative basis. Other types of objectives must be analyzed on the basis of what was accomplished relative to other years and perhaps to other companies.

Pillsbury:[a] Financial Goals and Objectives

The Pillsbury Company's financial goals and objectives are based upon measures of superior competitive performance.

Management believes these standards are appropriate guides for development of plans and evaluation of performance over time.

---

[a]Used by permission of the Pillsbury Company.

These goals include:

To earn the highest possible return on shareholders' equity consistent with responsible business practices;

To ensure repetitive, predictable and steadily growing per share profits and dividends as the yield from an ample stream of reinvestments; and

To perform consistently better than the industry in every market where Pillsbury products and services compete.

These goals translate into the following financial objectives:

Annual earnings per share growth of 12 to 15 percent.

Pretax return on average invested capital of 25 percent.

Aftertax return on average stockholders' equity of 18 percent.

A strong "A" credit rating on senior debt of the parent company.

Arizona Public Service Company[b]

CUSTOMER SERVICE AND PRODUCT QUALITY

To supply gas and electric service for the home, the community, commerce, agriculture, industry, and government:

at the lowest possible cost

in the quantities customers demand

with constantly improved quality

with increasing beneficial uses of our service

PROFITABILITY

To earn an adequate profit so that:

investors' risk and replacement and obsolescence of capital assets can be provided for

earnings can be reinvested and new capital can be attracted and retained

the company's total efforts and net effectiveness will be financially sound

EMPLOYEE ATTITUDES AND INCENTIVES

To attain skillful, safe performance, loyalty and teamwork of individual employees by

---

[b]Used by permission of the Arizona Public Service Company.

establishing good wages, benefits, and working conditions

maintaining security of employment

preserving individual human values and human dignity

assuring opportunity for self-improvement, advancement, and self-realization

MANAGERIAL PERFORMANCE AND DEVELOPMENT

To provide for a continuity of managerial leadership and company progress by:

stimulating continuous moral and technical self-development of managerial personnel

soundly designing a dynamic organization structure clearly defining objectives, policies, and standards of managerial performance

assuring opportunity and authority to perform within the bounds of capacities, objectives, and job functions

establishing incentives proportionate to responsibilities, risks, and results

PHYSICAL AND FINANCIAL RESOURCES

To provide for the future financial and physical needs of the company by planning and providing for

continuing sources of adequate fuel and power

adequate office facilities, tools, and equipment

capital supply requirements

PRODUCTIVITY

To attain constantly improving productive performance of all employees through

effective and balanced utilization of human and material resources

development and adoption of new tools, equipment, and methods, and through refinement of proven methods of work

feasible but challenging standards of performance for individual employees and each segment of the organization

INNOVATION AND RESEARCH

To engage in research and study in all fields and areas of work relating to business and the utility industry by

contributing to, developing, and utilizing technological advances developing sensitivity to changing conditions—economic, technological, and scientific developing new, better, and more efficient methods of rendering service to customers

keeping up with advances in knowledge and skills in all major areas of activity

PUBLIC RESPONSIBILITY

To recognize the company's public responsibility and earn public confidence by

leading in efforts to bring about community and industrial growth, development and betterment

opposing efforts to destroy individual initiative and the private business system

maintaining constructive and forthright relationships with governmental bodies

contributing to the development and strength of the utility and allied industries, sharing our advances and benefiting from experience and ideas

Corporate Strategies

The final stage in the strategic planning process is the development of the overall corporate strategies that will be used to accomplish objectives.

Designing strategies involves: (1) identifying strategic options, (2) assessing the options, and (3) selecting the strategy or strategies.

Identifying Market Opportunities

Before a strategy is selected, opportunities must be identified and defined. The rest of this chapter discusses a useful approach to identifying opportunities. The exact nature of opportunities is discussed in detail in chapters 3 through 6.

Basic Growth Strategies

Since most companies consider *growth* one of their basic objectives, one area of strategy development concerns the question of how to obtain growth. There are three possible alternative growth strategies:

1. Product/market expansion strategies
2. Integrative strategies
3. Diversification strategies

These strategic alternatives can be illustrated in a 2 × 2 matrix called a product/market growth matrix, as illustrated in figure 2–2.

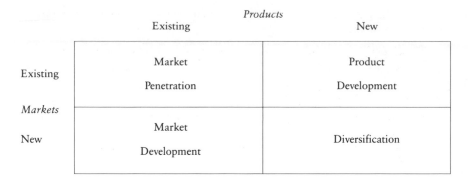

Products

	Existing	New
Existing Markets	Market Penetration	Product Development
New	Market Development	Diversification

Source: Adapted from H. Igor Ansoff, "Strategies for Diversification," *Harvard Business Review*, September–October 1957, pp. 113–124.

Figure 2–2. Product/Market Growth Matrix

Product/Market Expansion Strategies. Product/market expansion strategies include growth through expansion of existing product markets, development of new products aimed at existing markets, and development of new markets for existing products. Each of these strategic options has its advantages and its risks for management. In a market penetration strategy, for example, management has the advantage of both product knowledge and knowledge of existing markets. The obvious disadvantage is the fact that the products will eventually pass through various product life-cycle stages, ending with sales decline and extinction.

In a product development strategy, management's advantage lies in knowledge of the market, since the products are aimed at existing markets. The disadvantage is lack of product knowledge. When a market development strategy is used, product knowledge is the advantage and lack of market knowledge the disadvantage. When a diversification strategy is undertaken, management is under the greatest strain. Lacking both product knowledge and market knowledge, they must either acquire this knowledge quickly or must acquire managers or companies who already have this product/market knowledge.

Market penetration involves growth through increasing sales of existing products in existing markets. This expansion of sales can come about by: (1) altering purchase patterns of existing customers—getting them to buy more when they purchase or to purchase more frequently, (2) attracting nonusers to purchase the product and (3) attracting purchasers of competitor's products to switch, thereby increasing market share. Alternatives 1 and 2 involve increasing the total size of the market; alternative 3 involves increasing market share.

Product development means increasing sales by introducing new products to existing markets. Product development involves altering products by:

(1) adding new features, (2) offering different quality levels, or (3) offering different sizes of the product.

Market development entails offering existing products to new markets—either new geographical markets, such as foreign countries, or new market segments not currently using the product.

Integrative Strategies. A company can choose as a strategic alternative growth through integration of activities within its current industry. There are three alternatives for this type of growth: (1) forward integration, (2) backward integration, and (3) horizontal integration.

Forward integration means the company looks "down" the channel of distribution to the next members of the channel, who currently represent a customer type. For example, a manufacturer who looks down the channel sees either wholesalers or retailers as the next channel member. Thus forward integration takes the form of expanding—either internally or through acquisitions—by taking over wholesaling or retailing functions.

Backward integration seeks growth through ownership of companies "up" channel—in other words, suppliers of products or raw materials. A manufacturer of automotive tires that builds its own plant to produce synthetic fibers used in tire production would be growing through backward integration.

Horizontal integration seeks growth through ownership of competitors. This strategy involves identifying and acquiring firms that are in competition with the firm seeking growth.

Diversification Strategies

A final strategic alternative for growth is *diversification*. Diversification entails introducing new products into new markets or acquiring other firms that are already in these new product/market situations. Diversification strategies can take various forms. The most common are: (1) product/technology-related, (2) market-related, and (3) non-product/nonmarket-related.

Product/technology-related diversification consists of adding products that are technologically related to existing products but are aimed at different markets. For example, a company that manufactures electronic watches for the consumer market might develop a line of industrial gauges using the same electronic technology.

Market-related diversification consists of introducing products aimed at the same market but using different product technologies. A company that manufactures and markets a line of cosmetics, for example, could introduce a cosmetic bag—a product aimed at the same market as cosmetics but involving a very different technology.

Non-product/nonmarket-related diversification, sometimes called *conglomerate* diversification, seeks to add new products aimed at new classes of customers. The family-oriented entertainment company referred to earlier is an example of this type of diversification. They introduced a new water-related recreation park aimed at the nontourist market, whereas their previous business efforts had been concentrated on non-water-related entertainment appealing to the tourist market.

Each of the growth strategies described here provides alternatives for a company seeking growth. Although each type was treated as a separate strategic alternative, it is possible to pursue more than one strategy at the same time, given the managerial and financial resources needed for such growth.

Strategies for Existing SBUs

The Boston Consulting Group, a well-known consulting organization, has developed an approach to strategic planning that classifies SBUs on the basis of their relative market share and growth potential. This approach, depicted in figure 2–3, permits development of strategies for each SBU based on its classification within the matrix.

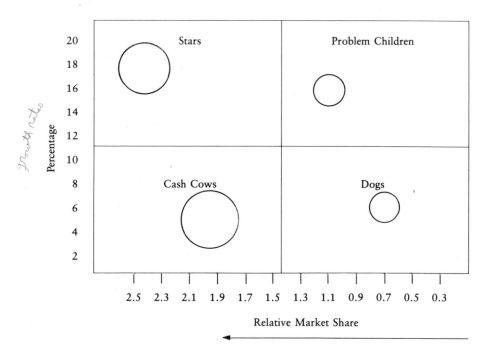

Source: Adapted from B. Hedley, "Strategy and the 'Business Portfolio,' " *Long Range Planning*, February 1977, p. 12.

Figure 2–3. Boston Consulting Group Business Portfolio Matrix

The vertical axis shows annualized market growth rates for each SBU in its respective market. The division between high and low rates at 10 percent is arbitrary.

The horizontal axis shows the market share of each SBU in relation to the industry leaders. Thus it is *relative*, not absolute, market share. If relative market share for an SBU is 1.5, it means that that SBU is the market leader and its share is one and one-half times greater than that of its nearest competitor. A relative market share of 0.8 would indicate that the SBU's market share was 80 percent of the market leader's share. Relative market share positions each SBU in relation to the leader and provides more information about market position than would absolute market share. The division at 1.5 is again an arbitrary point for separating SBUs into high and low relative market shares.

The size of the circle represents the proportional dollar contribution of each SBU to total company sales. The larger the circle, the larger that SBU's contribution to total company sales.

Given this information, each SBU is placed in one of the four quadrants resulting in the following four classifications of SBUs:

1. *Cash cows:* A cash cow is an SBU with a high relative market share compared to other competitors in the market, but in an industry that has a low annual growth rate. These SBUs generate more than enough cash to cover operating expenses, and their industry growth rate does not warrant large investments in that industry. The cash generated can therefore be used to support other SBUs that offer more potential for growth.

2. *Stars:* Stars are those SBUs that have a high relative market share and are also in an industry with expected high rates of growth. Their high growth rates usually represent high demand for cash to finance their growth.

3. *Problem children:* Problem children are those SBUs that have a low relative market share but are in industries with high annual rates of growth. They have the potential to become stars, but their low relative share represents a major challenge to management to create strategies capable of increasing relative market share.

4. *Dogs:* Dogs are SBUs that not only have low relative market share but also are in industries with low growth potential. They may not be operating at a loss, but they generate only enough cash to maintain their operations and market share.

Classifying a company's SBUs into such a matrix helps define the current position of each SBU and also suggests strategic options for management to improve performance. Although the position of an SBU will change over time because of changes in growth rates or market position, the following four strategic actions are implied for the four cells: (1) "milk" cows, (2) "shine" stars, (3) "solve" problems, and (4) "shoot" dogs.

1. *Milk cows:* The strategy for cash cows is to spend enough on them to maintain their market share ("keep them healthy") so they can continue to generate cash.

2. *Shine stars:* The strategy for stars is to continue to invest funds into these SBUs to support their growth rate and high market shares. They will eventually slow in growth, becoming cash cows themselves and helping to generate funds for new stars.

3. *Solve problems:* The strategy for these SBUs involves one of two options: (1) develop and test strategies for improving market share, or (2) divest of these SBUs and use the cash for supporting other more promising SBUs.

4. *Shoot dogs:* These SBUs, with their low market share and low growth potential, are prime prospects for divestiture. Cash generated by divesting of these SBUs can be reinvested in other SBUs with more potential.

Summary

This chapter has provided an overview of the strategic planning process that is the foundation for market opportunity analysis. As management goes through the process of strategic planning, each strategic option must be viewed as an opportunity that must be carefully analyzed before a given option is selected. Thus opportunity analysis is a prerequisite for successful strategic moves by a company.

The following chapters are designed to provide a detailed examination of the procedures and tools that can be used to complete the opportunity analysis. Opportunity analysis begins with an analysis of market demand, which is the subject of the next two chapters.

Notes

1. See Philip Kotler, *Marketing Management: Analysis, Planning, and Control* (Englewood Cliffs, N.J.: Prentice-Hall, 1980), p. 64.

2. See Derek F. Abell, "Strategic Windows," *Journal of Marketing* (Chicago), July 1978, pp. 21–26.

3. Kotler, *Marketing Management Analysis*, p. 76.

4. See Peter F. Drucker, *Management: Tasks, Responsibilities, Practices,* (New York: Harper and Row, 1974), p. 75.

5. Ibid.

6. Colowyo Coal Company, *Colowyo Magazine* (Meeker, Colo.), Spring 1980, p. 1. Used by permission.

7. See Drucker, *Management*, p. 101.

Part II
External Analysis

3
Market Demand Analysis

nalysis of market demand involves: (1) identifying a market, (2) identifying market factors, (3) estimating market potential, and (4) estimating anticipated revenues from a given venture. This chapter examines three of these four steps. The procedures for estimating revenues are discussed in chapter 5 after the analysis of competition's impact on a given market is discussed in chapter 4.

Identifying a Market

One fundamental concept underlying the type of analysis described in this chapter is that what is sometimes referred to as a market for a product or service is actually a composite of smaller markets, each with identifiable characteristics. When we speak of the automobile market, for example, we are referring to a large market that comprises smaller submarkets or segments. This market can be segmented in several ways to identify the various submarkets. The size of the car different consumers want, for example, could be used to identify at least four submarkets or segments: full-size, intermediate, compact, and subcompact. This process of breaking up a market into its constituent parts is usually referred to as *market segmentation*. The premise is that the consumers in one market are different from the consumers in another market and therefore each represents a separate entitly.

The rationale for market segmentation lies in the fact that markets are too complex and diverse for all consumers within the market to be considered homogeneous. If a new product or service is designed to appeal to teenagers, for example, then that segment or part of the total market between the ages of thirteen and nineteen is the market of interest. Its size and characteristics must be identified and studied, not those of the other segments.

Bases for Market Segmentation

There are several commonly used bases for segmentation, including geographic, demographic, product use, and product benefits. A discussion of the use of market grids is presented in this section to show how several of the bases can be combined for analysis and construction of individual market segments.

Geographic and Demographic Segmentation

The most commonly used basis for segmentation involves geographic and demographic variables. *Geographic* segmentation uses census tracts, cities, trade areas, counties, states, regions, and countries as the basis of segmentation. For many products, this is a logical framework. Snowmobiles, for example, will be purchased only in areas with sufficient snowfall.

Demographic segmentation involves the use of variables such as sex, age, income, and educational level as a basis for segmenting a market. In the market grids used in the following section, age and sex are used as two variables to segment the clothing market. These variables are appropriate for many products and services.

Geographic and demographic characteristics of industrial consumers can also be useful in segmenting industrial markets. In fact, some customers are concentrated both geographically and by industry in certain industrial markets. Tire manufacturers in Ohio and electronics manufacturers in California are two examples.

Segmentation by Product Use

A recent approach to market segmentation concentrates on the product use patterns of consumers as the basis for segmentation.

Consumers are classified as *users* and *nonusers*; users are further classified as *light, medium,* and *heavy* users. In some product categories (for example, air travel, car rentals, dog food purchases, and hair coloring purchases) a small percentage of the consumers accounts for a majority of the purchases. Usage rates become important as a basis for segmentation for such products.

Benefit Segmentation

Another way to segment markets is on the basis of the benefits the buyers expect to receive upon purchasing or using a product. In one study, the toothpaste market was segmented on such bases as flavor and product appearance, brightness of teeth, decay prevention, and price. Each of these variables represents the principal benefits sought by the purchaser. Each of these benefit segments in turn is composed of consumers with different demographic characteristics, personalities, life-styles, and so on. Thus each represents a distinct market segment.

Market Grids

One basic tool that can be used to segment a market is a market grid. A market grid is a two-dimensional view of a market, which is divided into various segments using *characteristics of potential consumers. Two important concepts in grid analysis are that characteristics of potential consumers* are used to segment the market rather than *product* characteristics. This ensures a market-oriented view of the market rather than a product-oriented view. Also, characteristics of *potential* consumers rather than *existing* consumers are used in order to focus on consumers whom the firm may not currently serve.

A series of grids must normally be used to completely describe a market. You must begin with a set of characteristics thought to be useful in differentiating consumers. Each characteristic must be analyzed to determine its probable effect on a market. The characteristics normally include geographic, socioeconomic, behavioral, and psychological dimensions. The objective is to isolate a specific market rather than a general one. Most products or services are not consumed by just anyone; the people or companies that are most likely to consume an offering must be identified.

Once a list of potential consumer characteristics has been developed, the next step is actual grid construction. Figures 3–1 and 3–2 show two grids for shoes. Each section within the grid is actually a market segment for shoes. Notice that as each characteristic is used to identify a specific segment, it becomes possible to begin to describe a market, which in turn permits collecting data on a specific market. These grids illustrate the *breakdown* approach to market segmentation, where the total market is broken up into various submarkets.

The two shaded areas in the first grid represent two completely different market segments. The styles of shoes desired, the emphasis on style, the types of stores where these consumers would prefer to shop, their buying motives—all these would normally be quite different and would represent different markets.

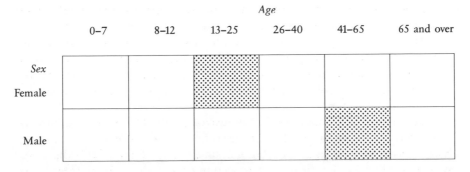

Figure 3–1. Grid 1 for Shoes

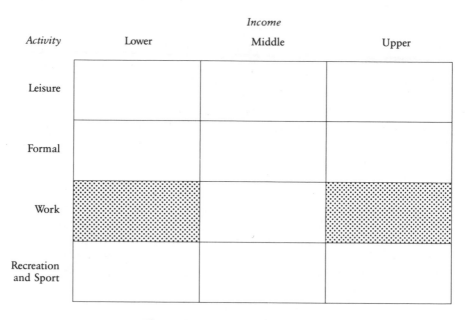

Figure 3–2. Grid 2 for Shoes

In the second grid, it also becomes apparent that the consumers represented by the two shaded areas (segments) represent different markets. You wouldn't expect a sanitation worker and a bank president to need the same type of shoes for work; likewise, they may not shop at the same retail outlets. A market segment represents a potential group of consumers with similar characteristics that define a market. For smaller companies, only one or a few segments may be of interest, whereas a large firm may develop or may already have a complete line of products or services and therefore may select several segments as potential target markets. Whether one or many segments are selected, this type of analysis is needed.

Some of the types of characteristics for consumer and industrial markets that may serve as a basis for segmentation are shown in table 3–1.

An alternative approach to developing a grid or diagram to represent a market would be a buildup approach. This approach involves identifying the individual market segments and then putting the segments together to represent a market. The result is the same—a recognition of the differences in needs of different consumers.

This approach is often used for industrial products. One project involved the reconstruction of the market for the component parts that make up "down hole equipment" used on oil rigs. The consumer analysis showed that the market was dominated by one firm, which accounted for about 80 percent of the original equipment market (OEM) sales in this market, with the rest of the

Table 3–1
Consumer Characteristics by Consumer Type

| Characteristic | Consumer Type | |
	Ultimate Consumers	*Industrial*
Socioeconomic	Age	Size—volume
	Sex	Number of employees
	Income	Number of plants
	Occupation	
	Education	Type of organization
	Marital status	Industry
Behavioral	Brands purchased	Decision-making patterns
	Coupon redemption	Growth potential
	Store shopped	Public versus private
	Loyalty	Distribution pattern
Psychological[a]	Attitudes	Management attitudes
	Personality traits	Management awareness
	Awareness	Management style
	Recall	Management values
	Hobbies	
	Reading interest	

[a]These would include psychographic characteristics.

sales volume going to several other firms. The large manufacturer was designated a *key account*, meaning it was considered a distinct segment of the market. All other accounts were put in a separate segment which contained only small accounts.

Market Factors

Market factors are those realities in the market that cause the demand for the product. For example, the market factor for baby beds is the number of babies born each year. Since a market is merely people with money and a motivation to buy, population figures and income figures are commonly used as market factors. However, it is usually possible to be much more specific in identifying market factors for a given company or a given product or service. The interest in market factors is threefold: (1) to identify the factors that influence demand for a product or service, (2) to determine the relationship between the factor and the product or service, and (3) to forecast that market factor for future years. Since many of the same market factors are used by different forecasters, much of the forecasting work may have already been completed and simply needs to be located. Population projections, for example, are available through many sources, so there is seldom any need to develop your own population forecast. Potential sources of data are given in appendix A.

Two basic techniques that are available for selecting and determining the impact of market factors on a given product or service are *arbitrary judgment* and *correlation analysis.* Arbitrary judgment uses the decision maker's own experience and judgment in selecting and weighing factors. (For new products or services this is a common technique, since no sales history is available unless, of course, a test market is used.) For example, a drug manufacturer might determine from historical data that $2 worth of drugs are purchased for each person residing in a given market area. The number of consumers in a market area would be used to get information on the future size of that market area.

A more complex but usually more reliable approach is to use correlation analysis to help identify factors and assign weights to them. Although it is not appropriate to discuss the details of this technique here, there is a specific technique in correlation analysis called stepwise regression analysis that not only weights the various factors but also provides a measure of what the addition of each factor would add to an explanation of changes in sales. Because this method requires a sales history, it is limited mainly to existing products, although it could be used on test market data for new products.

Regardless of the technique used in analyzing market factors, the basic information sought deals with understanding the factors that influence demand for a product or service and the historical and future trend for each factor. This will be more evident in the discussion of the use of market factors to estimate market potential in the next section.

Market Potential

Once a market has been divided into various segments and characteristics of consumers and the market factors in each market have been analyzed, the next step is to estimate the size of the market. The term *market potential* is used to refer to the expected sales of a product or service for an entire market—the answer to the question: "If everyone who could buy would buy, how many units or dollars worth of sales would occur?" A market segment that does not have enough consumers spending enough dollars does not justify effort in that market unless a firm is seeking to accomplish some non-revenue-related objective. You are seeking not just consumer markets but markets that can be served profitably by the firm attempting to meet their needs. Market potential is a quantitative measure of a market's capacity to consume a product in a given time period—a prerequisite to assessing profitability.

Estimating Potential for Existing Products

Market potential can be measured in either absolute or relative terms. An absolute measure is one that can be expressed in units or dollars; a relative measure relates one part of a market to another and is expressed as a percentage. This section presents one technique for estimating relative potential and two techniques for estimating absolute potential. These techniques are used when products and services are already on the market and an estimate of the future size of the market is desired.

The Sales Index Measure of Relative Potential. The sales index method provides a relative measure of potential for products that have reached maturity in their product life cycle. This technique is useful in answering questions about the relative potential of various geographical market areas. Its use requires familiarity with the product's stage and life cycle, with penetration of distribution in various areas, and with the product's sales history.

This technique is illustrated in table 3–2. Notice that the resulting figures are percentages of total industry sales by region. This says, in effect, that industry sales will occur next year in the same proportion as last year's in each region. The potential in the northwest region is expected to be 23.2 percent of the total—whatever that total turns out to be next year. One region can be compared to another using this measure of potential.

The Market Factor Method. Normally, relative potential is inadequate; an absolute measure of potential is needed to provide estimates of potential in units or dollars. One technique used to accomplish this is the market factor method. This involves identifying the factors that influence a good or service's sales and relating the factor to sales in some way. This was mentioned in the previous chapter. An example of this method is shown in table 3–3, in which population is used as the market factor. Population, the market factor, is related to sales in this example through the sales rate or dollars of sales per 1,000 people. Notice that absolute and relative potential could be calculated by region by using the projected regional population as the factor and the regional sales rate to relate sales to the market factor in each region.

It should be apparent that, given a market segment, the number of people in that segment, and an expenditure rate, the potential of that segment can be calculated. Using this technique produces an estimate of the absolute

Table 3–2
Soft Contact Lens: Sales Index Method

Region	Industry Sales	Sales Index	Potential
Northeast	$ 8,500,009	28.8%	28.8%
Southeast	6,753,090	22.8	22.8
Northwest	6,870,421	23.2	23.2
Southwest	7,430,218	25.2	25.2
	$29,553,738	100.0%	100.0%

Source: Artificial data.

Table 3–3
The Market Factor Method

Region	Sales ($) 1980	Population (000)	Sales Rate/1,000
Northeast	$ 8,500,009	68,570	$123.96
Southeast	6,753,090	38,720	174.40
Northwest	6,870,421	32,810	209.40
Southwest	7,430,218	66,730	111.34
	$29,553,738	206,830	$154.78 average

Notes: Population projection (1981) = 210,847,000; sales rate (average) = $154.78 per 1,000; potential (154.78 × 210,847) = $32,634,898.

potential of a given market. This technique would be appropriate when an established market is being evaluated.

The Regression Analysis Method

Another technique for estimating potential involves the use of a statistical technique known as regression analysis. This technique still uses market factors, but these market factors are related to sales in a more mathematically complex manner. Space does not permit a complete explanation of this technique. The purpose here is to show how it could be used in estimating potential. One result of regression analysis is an equation that relates the market factor to sales. If more than one market factor is used, then multiple regression is needed. Table 3–4 shows data that have been analyzed using two market factors. The resulting equation is then used to estimate potential. This approach still requires estimates of the two market factors (independent variables) for the future time period for which the measure of potential is desired. In this example, Y represents total industry sales; X_1 and X_2 represent two market factors that are related to total industry sales. Estimates of the value of these factors for the next time period are substituted into the equation to calculate estimate of industry potential. This technique also permits calculation of a confidence interval for the estimate.

Estimating Potential for New Products or Services

When innovative products or services are proposed, no industry sales history is available as a point of reference for estimating potential. Under such circumstances, it is still important to identify market factors that are likely to influence the demand for the product or service. These factors can provide an upper limit to demand. The knowledge that there are five million men in a certain income and age category would provide a useful reference point in beginning to analyze potential for a new product for males with these two characteristics. However, you would not expect every one of them to buy the product.

Table 3–4
Estimating Market Potential Using Multiple Regression Analysis

Year	Industry Sales (thousands) Y	Factor 1 (thousands) X_1	Factor 2 (thousands) X_2
1973	6,860	1,329	40
1974	6,520	1,116	39
1975	6,345	1,041	40
1976	6,710	1,209	37
1977	7,222	1,553	44
1978	6,810	1,296	45
1979	7,005	1,365	44
1980	7,275	1,492	50
1981	7,450	1,641	53
1982	7,250	1,591	59
1983	7,105	1,510	66
1984	6,666	1,196	71
1985	6,900	1,322	72

Notes: $Y = a + b_1X_1 + b_2X_2$ (general equation).
   $Y = 4,641 + (1.70)(1,600) + (-.46)(60)$.
   $Y = 7,333.4$, the estimated market potential for this product.

Three techniques commonly used to refine estimates of potential from that up-per limit are: (1) judgmental estimates, (2) consumer surveys, and (3) the substitute method. A fourth technique combines several techniques and uses secondary data and consumer surveys to estimate potential.

(1) **Judgmental Estimates.** This involves the use of expert opinions of those who are knowledgeable about the market and the product. This judgment can be used in a formalized approach such as the Delphi technique, or it can involve pooled estimates and a reconciliation of difference between estimates given by different people.

(2) **Consumer Surveys.** Surveys of potential consumers can be used to estimate the market for potential new products. This approach is especially useful for industrial products, where there are fewer consumers and they can be more readily identified. For example, a part used in mud pumps for oil drilling rigs would be sold to only a few customers—manufacturers of mud pumps—who can be easily identified and their potential purchases of the part estimated. Although the more diverse consumer market makes this technique more dif-ficult to use, it can be adapted to consumer goods.

(3) **Substitute Method.** Most new products are substitutes for products already on the market. If the size of the markets for these existing products can be estimated, then the sales of the new product can be estimated on the basis of

Table 3–5
Market Potential for an Ironing Board Attachment in the Southeastern United States

State	Number of Households (thousands)[a]	Number Who Own Ironing Boards (thousands)[b]	Number Who Use Spray Starch/Sizing (thousands)[c]	Number Who Experience Problems (thousands)[d]	Number Likely To Buy (thousands)[e]	Market Potential[f]	
						Units	Dollars
Alabama	1,342	1,288.3	876.0	473.0	184.5	184,500	$ 784,125
Arkansas	816	783.4	532.7	287.7	112.2	112,200	476,850
Florida	3,744	3,594.2	2,444.1	1,319.8	712.7	712,700	3,028,975
Georgia	1,872	1,797.1	1,222.0	659.9	257.4	257,400	1,093,950
Kentucky	1,263	122.5	824.5	445.2	173.7	173,700	738,225
Louisiana	1,412	1,355.5	921.7	497.7	194.1	194,100	824,925
Mississippi	827	793.9	539.7	291.4	113.6	113,600	482,800
North Carolina	2,043	1,961.3	1,333.7	720.2	280.9	280,900	1,193,825
South Carolina	1,030	988.8	672.4	363.1	141.6	141,600	601,800
Tennessee	1,619	1,554.3	1,056.9	570.7	222.6	222,600	945,050
Virginia	4,452	4,273.9	2,906.3	1,569.4	612.1	612,100	2,601,425
West Virginia	1,705	1,636.8	1,113.0	601.0	234.4	234,400	996,200

[a]Source: U.S. Census of Population, 1980.
[b]From *The Consumer Survey*, 96 percent.
[c]From *The Consumer Survey*, 68 percent.
[d]From *The Consumer Survey*, 54 percent.
[e]From *The Consumer Survey*, 39 percent.
[f]An expected median price of $4.25 based on data from the consumer study was used to calculate market potential.

its replacement potential for some existing product or products. An acceptance rate would have to be estimated for the proportion of existing consumers that would switch to the new product when it was introduced on the market. This acceptance rate could be estimated through consumer research.

An example of the use of combined techniques to estimate potential for a new product is shown in the following paragraphs. This example, based on actual data, shows how data from several sources can be combined to estimate market potential.

The purpose of the analysis was to evaluate the market potential for a new consumer product used in ironing. This involved evaluation of total market size and acceptance levels for this product.

To accomplish these objectives, to separate phases of the study were completed. *Phase I* was the market potential analysis based on data collected from secondary sources to estimate total market size. *Phase II* of the study was a consumer survey of homemakers. This survey involved collecting data from a random sample of 100 homemakers to permit more precise estimates of market potential for the product, thereby reducing the risks involved in introducing the product.

Data for the consumer study were collected by telephone interviewers. The resulting data were analyzed using a computer to develop cross-tabulations of the responses. This permitted comparisons of consumers on various characteristics to assess product acceptance.

It was assumed that the consumer study respondents, though not representative of the total United States, were representative of consumers in the Southeast, since the data were collected in that region. Market potential for the southeastern United States was estimated by state, as shown in table 3–5.

For this twelve-state area, market potential was 3,239,800 units. If the expected price most commonly mentioned in the consumer study were the actual market price, this would produce a market potential estimate of $13,769,150 in retail sales for this region of the United States.

As this example indicates, the data collected in the consumer study were used to refine the estimates of market potential. Instead of assuming all households used ironing boards and had experienced the problems the new product would alleviate, data were collected. This permitted eliminating consumers who didn't have an ironing board, didn't use spray starch, didn't experience specific problems, or said that would not be likely to buy the product if it was available. The price they would expect to pay enabled those preparing the study to estimate potential in units and dollars.

Summary

The analysis of markets discussed in this chapter lays the foundation for the analysis to be discussed in later chapters. An understanding of the market and the factors that influence the growth and size are fundamental concepts for any opportunity.

This foundation is expanded in the next chapter as competitors are analyzed with respect to specific product-market situations. Competitive conditions not only influence the nature of the opportunity but also provide examples of potentially successful strategies.

4
Competitive Analysis

After analyzing environmental factors, market factors, potential, and consumer needs in specific market segments, the next step in market opportunity analysis is to analyze competition for each specific market segment. For new products that represent innovations, this analysis may be limited to potential competition rather than identifiable competitors. In most cases, however, an established market exists, with clearly identified competitors who must be evaluated for their strategies, strengths, and weaknesses.

This chapter presents the concepts and tools needed to analyze competition for existing markets. Especially useful is the marketing mix audit form, which permits evaluation of a competitor in all the basic strategy elements.

Purpose of Competitive Analysis

In undertaking competitive analysis, one fundamental question is asked: *Which competitors are going after which market segments with what marketing strategies?* The focus again is on specific market segments that have been isolated through consumer analysis. At this point, you should already know the size (potential) and characteristics of each segment. Now the analysis begins to deal with competition on a segment-by-segment basis. You are trying to uncover segments that are not currently being served or segments that are not being served well by competitors. In markets where competitors have no clearly identifiable strategy and each seems to be using a strategy similar to that of the others, there are usually several segments that can be better served through strategies aimed directly at their needs.

Until the 1970s the hair shampoo market was characterized by two broad categories of shampoo—dandruff and nondandruff. Recognition of consumers' different hair and scalp conditions, however, led to the development of different shampoos for dry, oily, and normal hair. This was an attempt to meet the needs of consumers more precisely than had previously been done. Likewise, the introduction of a shampoo especially designed for small children was an attempt to meet a need not previously met well by any competitor.

Types of Competition

To be complete, the anlaysis of competition must consider both *existing* and *potential* competition. Trying to anticipate the competitor's moves can become the basis for deciding whether or not to pursue a given segment and what strategy to use if the effort is made. This chapter begins with a discussion of the nature of competition and then develops basic tools to analyze competitors.

Pure Competition

One of the earliest types of competition identified by economists is called pure competition. Although all the characteristics of this type of competition are seldom found in the marketplace, it is somewhat characteristic of some market environments and serves as a useful analytical concept. An industry or a local market that could be described as pure competition usually has the following characteristics: (1) large number of relatively small competitors, (2) little or no differences between strategies, (3) ease of entry by new competitors. The large number of small competitors means the actions of one competitor may be unnoticed by the others. Differences among strategies may be small, and good location may be of prime importance in attracting customers. The ease of entry may mean new competitors continually coming into the market or old ones leaving. Unless a well-financed competitor enters the market and alters the competitive environment, the market tends to be unorganized, even fragmented, with the number of customers and competitors within the geographical bounds of the firm determining both sales and strategies. Similarities in prices, products or services offered, distribution, and promotion are common.

Monopolistic Competition

In the market characterized by monopolistic competition, the individual images of the various firms begin to emerge in terms of more clearly differentiated strategies. Although there may still be many competitors and relative ease of entry, each firm has attempted to differentiate itself in some way from its competitors. It may be a market with much diversity of price, distribution, products and services, and promotional activities; or it may be characterized by similarities among two or three variables in the marketing mix and variety in the other—promotion, for example. In this competitive environment each competitor has more control over the marketing mix variables; therefore, a diversity of strategies is possible.

Oligopolistic Competition

In the competitive environment described as oligopolistic, the number of competitors and ease of entry are both decreased. In this market there are a few relatively large competitors and perhaps a few smaller ones. The actions of one competitor are clearly recognized in both nature and impact by other competitors, and their retaliation to competitive moves is anticipated. There is still a diversity of strategies in this type of environment, but it is most likely of the nonprice variety; price competition is not easily copied and must be responded to if customers readily substitute one firm's products for another. Price leadership may develop as one firm is allowed to set the pace for others.

Monopoly

A monopoly is a market environment characterized by one seller. There are usually legal restrictions to entry if it is considered a natural monopoly (such as a telephone company or an electric utility). Natural monopolies are regulated by government in terms of prices and distribution; nonnatural monopolies, if successful, usually attract other competitors who are willing to overcome barriers to entry because of a potentially large return. Therefore, nonnatural monopolies are usually short-lived.

Level of Competition

One important aspect of competition is the level at which it is analyzed. At the manufacturing level, there may be only a few large producers (oligopoly) but many retailers reselling the products in highly competitive markets (monopolistic or purely competitive). Therefore, the planner must analyze the market in terms of where his or her own firm faces competition. If the marketing plan is being developed for a retail firm, the retail market is of prime consideration, whereas a manufacturer may be more concerned about competition at the manufacturing level.

In some instances it may be appropriate to look at competition vertically, with one channel system competing with another channel system, rather than only horizontally. This would be especially true where vertical integration is involved.

Deciding on the Nature of the Competition

Table 4–1 provides a summary of how several factors vary depending on the type of competitive environment that is appropriate. This chart is useful in understanding the nature of the competitive environment. Instead of trying to define what is meant by "many" (in the case of number of firms) or "ease of entry" (in the case of how easy it is to enter a market), attention should be focused on the overall nature of the market as described by these factors *collectively*. Since most economic reality lies somewhere between pure competition

Table 4–1
Effects of Competitive Environment

Factor	Competitive Environment			
	Pure Competition	Monopolistic Competition	Oligopolistic Competition	Monopoly
Number of firms	Many	Many	Few	One
Entry and exit	Easy	Easy	Difficult	May be legally banned.
Product	Undifferentiated	Differentiated	Differentiated	Not applicable (NA)
Price	Undifferentiated	Undifferentiated if nonprice competition is emphasized.	Undifferentiated if nonprice competition is emphasized.	
		Differentiated if price competition is used by some competitors.	Differentiated if price competition is used by some competitors.	
Place	Undifferentiated	Differentiated if nonprice competition is used by some competitors.	Differentiated if nonprice competition is used by some competitors.	NA
		Undifferentiated if price competition is emphasized.	Undifferentiated if price competition is emphasized.	
Promotion	Undifferentiated	Differentiated if nonprice competition is used by some competitors.	Differentiated if nonprice competition is used by some competitors.	NA
		Undifferentiated if price competition is emphasized.	Undifferentiated if price competition is emphasized.	
Competitive reactions	Little	Some, depending on type of action.	A lot, especially price action.	NA

and monopoly, analytical attention should be focused there. Identifying the nature of competition helps in understanding not only how firms compete in a market but also whether or not retaliatory actions can be expected.

Competitive Advantages

Effective competitive anlaysis will take into consideration the search for—and need for—differential advantages. Differential advantages are those factors in which a particular organization excels over competitive organizations or has the potential to excel over them. Some strategic planners actually insist that a result of the strategic planning process must be some differential advantage for the organization. Differential advantages may be found in the areas of (1) production, (2) technology, (3) natural resources, (4) marketing, and (5) management.

Production: A superior ability to turn out a product is a crucial differential advantage that many companies have capitalized on. The advantage may also lie in a firm's ability to maintain superior production quality over its competitors.

Technology: Initial innovative research and development, as well as properly managed scientific application, can establish and preserve strong differential advantages over competitors.

Natural resources: Valuable or scarce resources are often appropriate assets on which to base a strategy. Tremendous advantage can be given to organizations, cartels, and nations that control natural resources or are located in favorable proximity to them.

Marketing: Market advantage usually refers to the advantage one firm has over another because it is more positively positioned in the minds of customers. Those firms having greater customer awareness, higher preference, or stronger loyalty have distinct marketing differential advantage over their competitors.

Management: Management advantage takes the form of positive personnel relations, effective planning and information systems, and overall managerial competence.

Industry Analysis

Part of the competitive analysis process is discovering differential advantages that will strengthen the strategy of the firm. To discover these differences, one must understand how the industry functions. Four key questions are helpful in conducting an industry analysis:

1. What are the strategically relevant aspects of the industry's structure?
2. In what direction is the industry headed and what forces are driving it in that direction?
3. What are the underlying economics of the industry, most particularly what must a firm know and do well to make money in this business?
4. What are the strategic issues and problems facing the industry?[1]

Analysis of *industry structure* involves determining the number of competitors, establishing their size relative to the total market, profiling the market leaders, analyzing distribution channels, developing consumer profiles, and evaluating ease of entry and exit as well as other characteristics.

Once the industry framework is understood, the analysis turns torward determining *industry direction*. Most industries go through an industry life cycle consisting of four stages: development, growth, maturity, and decline. This model of understanding and predicting industry direction is not always accurate, however. Some industries go through several cycles. The checklist in table 4–2 includes many of the considerations required to answer the question of where the industry is going and what is driving it that way.

There are many other driving forces not listed here. Various industries have different forces that come into play in determining the direction of the industry, and these forces have different magnitudes of importance from one industry to another.

The forces of competition greatly influence an organization's strategy formation and market opportunity decisions (see figure 4–1). Although each industry has its own unique characteristics, five main forces represent the actual driving mechanisms of any given industry:[2]

1. The industry itself and the competitive decisions and activities engaged in by each company
2. The consumer/buyer composition
3. The supplier composition
4. The possibility of new entrants
5. The availability of good product substitutes

The *industry* and the individual companies within the industry are constantly involved in dynamic interplay in an attempt to build a successful competitive edge over one another. The success of one organization's strategy in accomplishing this is based in large measure on the strategies of the other members. Constant monitoring of these interdependent strategic maneuvers is required to make the adjustments necessary to improve competitive position and achieve market success.

The *consumer/buyer composition* can range from a few large-volume purchasers to a large number of low-volume purchasers. In the first instance, losing a few customers can be the difference between success and failure; at the other extreme losing the same number of customers has virtually no impact. Most firms try to minimize the number of customers that can exert an adverse effect on their business.

The *supplier composition* also has an important influence on the competing position of individual organizations. The relative importance of the goods or services they supply will determine the strength of their competitive influence

Table 4–2
Industry Evaluation Factors

Checklist

1. Growth	Slow	Medium	Fast
2. Customers	Growing	Declining	No Change
3. Technology	Low	Medium	High
4. Product change	Slow	Medium	Fast
5. Danger of obsolescence	Low	Medium	High
6. Ease of entry	Low	Medium	High
7. Quality of suppliers	Low	Medium	High
8. Possibility of regulatory changes	Low	Medium	High
9. Availability of raw materials/resources	Low	Medium	High
10. Amount of capital required	Low	Medium	High

over firms in the industry. They can have a positive or negative impact on profit margins, inventory levels, product quality, and prices.

The *possibility of new entrants* into the market constantly threatens to alter market share, production capacity, and supply distribution within the industry. This threat can be minimal when there are strong barriers to entry such as strong customer loyalty, large capital requirements, difficulty in establishing distribution channels, and strong response of current market participants. When entry barriers are weak or expected response of existing firms is weak, however, then the possibility of entry is stronger.

The fifth force in this five-force model is the *availability of good product substitutes*. There is a major threat to existing firms when high-quality substitutes exist in ample quantity at competitive or comparable prices. Artificial sweeteners and sugar are examples of substitutable products.

The third key question in a competitive analysis is: "What are the underlying economics of the industry?" The elements of an answer to this question are capital investment requirements, break-even levels, cost structures, pricing structures, and other economic considerations. The key factors related to the economic characteristics will be discussed in a later chapter. At this juncture, however, it should be established that the key success factors vary from industry to industry and an understanding of the economics of the industry is necessary

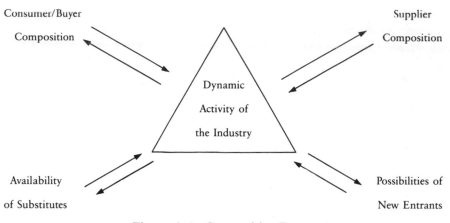

Figure 4–1. Competitive Forces

to take advantage of these factors. Whether it is transportation, distribution, promotion, technology, raw materials, location, or some other key element, an understanding of the underlying economic considerations increases the likelihood of selecting the key factors for success in the industry.

The fourth key question, listed earlier, was to identify the strategic issues and problems facing the industry. These issues and problems vary from time to time and from industry to industry. The following are the most common issues and problems within an industry:

1. Capability to meet future needs
2. Ability to estimate changes in the demographic characteristics of consumers
3. Capacity to deal with emerging opportunities and threats
4. Ability to trace the overall economy and estimate its impact on the industry
5. Ability to anticipate changes in government policies and regulatory controls
6. Capability to predict and respond to changes in supply, cost, competition, technology, growth, and so on

Competitor Analysis

Once a good understanding of how the industry functions is established, a specific competitor analysis comes next. Most firms in a given industry do not follow the same strategic approach, regardless of the similarity of their understanding of industry dynamics. Evaluating the competitors' strategy in the market allows a business entity to increase or reinforce its understanding of buyer behavior and to identify the type of customer to which it is appealing.

It is also useful in identifying strengths and weaknesses and, consequently, potential market opportunity. The analysis may assist the firm in evaluating whether to position itself as a *leader* competing head-on with other competitors, as a *follower* with a "me too" strategy, or as a *niche* performer with a unique strategy tailored to specific strengths and weaknesses and specific market segments.

In evaluating different competitive approaches, the following need to be considered:

Current strategy

Current performance

Strengths and weaknesses

Future strategic possibilities

Each major competitor should be studied separately. If this is not possible, then the strategy of the closest competitors should be evaluated.

Analyzing current competitor strategy involves determining how the competitor defines the industry in terms of market segments, product features, marketing mix, manufacturing policy, research and development commitment, growth policy, distribution, and promotion. This analysis can take several forms, but perhaps the most useful is the competitive market mix audit.

The Competitive Market Mix Audit

The competitive market mix audit is one of the best ways of evaluating the marketing performance of a company and its competitors.[3] Such an audit should be comprehensive, independent, periodic, and based on specific objectives. Once the objectives and scope of the audit are established, a data-gathering effort should be initiated. This data collection effort can be accomplished by an objective outside consultant or by an in-house staff or task force. The results of the audit should be a clear comparison of the company and its competitors showing relative strengths and weaknesses as well as opportunities and threats. Other possible outcomes include the detection of inappropriate objectives, obsolete strategies, ill-advised use of resources, and other reasons to revise the company's direction relative to competition.

The word *audit*, regardless of the business context in which it is used, refers to an unbiased appraisal of what is being done and how it is being done. Thus an accounting audit refers to an analysis of everything that is being done in the accounting area of a firm. Similarly, a competitive marketing mix audit is an analysis of competitors' activities by market segment. The form shown in table 4–3 is one of the most useful tools available for performing such an audit for a retail company. Other audit forms with different comparison

Table 4–3
Competitive Market Mix Audit Form

	Competitor A				Competitor B				Competitor C			
	–	?	0	+	–	?	0	+	–	?	0	+
Product or Service												
1. Customer acceptance												
2. Customer satisfaction in use												
3. Product quality level(s)/innovations												
4. Adequacy of assortments												
5. Services provided												
Place												
1. Customer accessibility												
2. Suitability of site												
3. Customer traffic potential												
4. Appearance of facility												
5. Selling areas												
6. Parking facilities												
7. Drawing power of neighboring firms												
8. Customer image of facilities												
Price												
1. Comparative price level(s)												
2. Consumers' images of store's prices												
3. Number of price lines												
4. Consistency of price policies												
5. Credit policies and practices												
Promotion												
1. Promotional ability												
2. Amount and quality of promotional efforts												
3. Ethical standards												
4. Consistency of efforts												

Note: The first symbol used, a minus sign, indicates that the business being evaluated ranks below the competitor on the specific factor; the second, a question mark, indicates that the relative standing is unknown; the third, a zero, indicates equal competitive standing; and the fourth, a plus sign, indicates that the business being evaluated ranks above the competition on the specific factor.

characteristics should be used for other industry categories. The audit involves the planner in an appraisal of every aspect of a firm's marketing mix compared to that of its major competitors. Several steps are involved in using this form to complete the audit.

First, the form should reflect the nature of the marketing mix activities for the type of firms being analyzed. For example, if retail firms are being analyzed, the form must reflect the components important in retailing. Specifically, place would be analyzed in terms of appearance, layout, and traffic flow throughout the stores. This analysis would not be appropriate for a manufacturer, since customers do not usually see the physical facility or move through it.

Second, the major competitors must be identified by name so that a realistic comparison can be made. This requirement forces the planner to identify the specific competitors for a particular market segment and permits the collection of data on those specific firms.

Third, sources of data must be identified to complete the audit. Some of the data may already by available from previous analysis or research and may merely need updating. Otherwise, data may have to be collected to complete the audit. For some types of comparisons, judgment must be used if research or other objective data are not available. There is a danger of a so-called halo effect surrounding what your firm is doing compared to its competitors. One way to avoid bias is to use the judgment of several people rather than relying on that of one person.

Finally, some system must be developed to grade your own company's effort and that of its competitors on each aspect of the audit. For new firms anticipating entry into a market, competitors are compared with each other. One ranking system is described at the bottom of table 4–3, where each competitor is ranked "higher," "lower," "equal to," or "don't know" on each part of the audit. Or you may prefer to rank competitors in order, using number 1 to indicate the best, number 2 the second best, and so on.

Rather than a more general analysis of price levels, this audit would have to be completed for *each segment* analyzed. The planner is not particularly interested in generalities here but, rather, in details about specific groups or market segments. Thoroughness is important in this type of analysis. A lack of details may be misleading.

In a consumer study done for a restaurant, respondents were asked whether they thought their friends would eat at that particular restaurant. If the answer was no, they were asked why. The most common response was that prices were "too high." Yet the competitive analysis shown in table 4–4 tells a completely different story. The prices charged by the Holliday Restaurant were about the same as those of the other competitors for comparable menu items, which means respondents only *thought* the prices were too high. This analysis leads to a completely different type of strategy or tactics than if prices were in fact higher than those of competitors.

Competitive Strategies and Resources

Several other factors should be analyzed for a more complete evaluation of competitors in a market. They include competitors' strategic tendencies and resources—marketing, financial, and production. These relate to long-run as opposed to short-run actions.

The first factor is concerned with competitors' willingness to change or react to competitive moves; the second deals with their ability to make strategic moves.

Assessing strategic tendencies involves deciding whether competitors' actions tend to be *reactive* or *proactive*. Reactive strategies are those that follow the

Table 4–4
Comparative Pricing: Restaurants

	8 ounce Rib Eye	Hamburger with Fries	Breakfast	Buffet	Banquet
Southern Inn	$7.26	$3.50	$1.95	$3.95/d.	$6.50
King's Inn	—	3.70	2.05	—	—
Charlie's Place	7.68	—	—	—	—
Tony's	6.84	3.25	1.75	—	5.25
Sandpiper	6.49	3.00	1.75	—	6.00
The Castle	7.96	3.60	1.85	—	On request
Ramble Inn	6.20	3.05	1.80	—	7.95
The Rib Joint	6.88	2.55	1.75	—	6.50–7.50
The Ice Box	7.16	3.40	—	—	6.50
Uncle Joe's	7.87	2.25	—	—	6.50
Captain Bill's	7.95	2.95	—	—	—
John's Diner	7.50	2.85	—	4.95/Sun.	6.35
				4.25/d.	6.35
Holliday Restaurant	7.25	2.75	1.95	4.95/Sun.	6.50
				3.95/d.	

Source: Artificial data.

lead of other firms in the market or simply settle into a niche. Proactive strategies involve market leadership or challenge to the market leaders. If market leaders and challengers can be identified, they are the competitors whose actions must be anticipated. The marketing mix audit of these firms helps identify the exact nature of their strategies in a short approach.

A strategy used by many firms in recent years is called *product positioning*—the placement of a product in terms of consumers' perceptions of it relative to other products. It is the answer to the question: "How do we want consumers to perceive our product relative to other products on the market?" The marketing mix is altered in an attempt to put that product in that position in the minds of consumers.

If the market for a product is viewed as a multidimensional plane, then all attributes of a product together make up its position. For simplicity, however, one or two key dimensions are usually chosen for analysis. When the Leeming/Pacquin Division of Pfizer, Inc., introduced Hai Karate, it was positioned to the right of Old Spice, Aqua Velva, and Mennen and to the left of Jade East and English Leather. Jade East and English Leather were at the high end of a price gap. Thus price and a unique advertising campaign were used to place Hai Karate between these two extremes, and the Hai Karate strategy was conceived in relation to competitive strategies.[4]

Assessing competitors' resources involves determining whether specific competitors have the marketing expertise to respond successfully to events in the marketplace; the productive capacity to respond in terms of both levels of demand and technology; and, finally, the financial resources to respond to problems and opportunities that occur. Moreover, since most firms attempt to build on their strengths and nullify their weaknesses, analysis can help them forecast the type of response they are most likely to make. A firm that is strong financially, with unused productive capacity but weaker marketing skills, is most likely to meet a challenge with lower prices or an increase in promotional expenditures than would a firm with an opposite set of strengths and weaknesses.

As the market moves toward oligopolistic competition, the need for this type of analysis increases. Failure to expect and anticipate competitive reactions means ignoring the realities of market dynamics.

After completing the competitive analysis by market segment, it is important to develop summary statements about each segment with respect to competition.

Search for a Differential Advantage

As each competitive firm's strategy, strengths, and weaknesses are analyzed for each market segment, the market analyst looks for those segments not being served or not being served well by the existing competition. Successful entry and exploitation of a marketing opportunity is much easier if a firm finds some differential advantage in the market.[5] *A differential advantage is one that gives one firm an edge over competitors and becomes a basis for differentiating one firm from another in the market.* The basis of the advantage could be price, product improvement, promotional appeals, product innovation, and so forth.

When this approach is used, the analyst begins interpreting "holes" in the market in terms of his or her own firm's ability to fill that niche. Thus opportunities and abilities are matched. This matching process is examined in more detail in chapter 7.

Positioning the Company/Product

Once you have adequately analyzed and assessed the competition, it is time to formulate the strategy to position your product, company, or strategic business unit on the basis of the competitive analysis. A company will probably be either a market leader, a market challenger, a market follower, or a market nicher.[6]

Market leaders are those that occupy first place by way of market share for a particular product or product line. Market leaders establish strategy to maintain their number one position. Their objectives usually are to expand total market usage of the product in order to protect their current market share. *Market challengers* are generally those firms occupying the second, third, or fourth place in market share (depending on the size of the market and the number of competitors). Though not as large as market leaders, these firms are usually quite large in their own right. Market challengers also seek to gain market share. They attempt to do this by frontal assaults or flanking movements specifically against the market leaders. Flanking strategies are generally preferred because they represent a concentration of effort against an identified area of weakness in the leader. Market challengers can also meet their objectives by attacking smaller competitors rather than the market leader. This is sometimes referred to as a *guppy strategy. Market followers* seldom choose to make frontal or head-on attacks on market leaders. Because of their smaller size and their less aggressive philosophy, market followers usually employ flanking or guppy strategies in the competitive area. *Market nichers* are smaller companies that appeal to a particular segment of the market on the basis of their unique strengths. Their strategies usually do not include head-on clashes with market leaders—or market challengers, for that matter. Market nichers usually capitalize on an area of specialization or specific market segment that large companies tend to overlook or ignore.

Successful positioning of a company or product, therefore, begins with an understanding of the company's market position in the competitive market as well as a broad-based knowledge of the company's strengths, weaknesses, and capabilities. This allows the company to stake out a position that will lead to long-term growth. Often this will require making product innovations, creating positive relationships with key suppliers and customers, establishing consumer awareness, and developing internal efficiencies and competence.

Summary

At this point in the analysis, the analyst should begin to see several clear-cut problems and opportunities in the market. Not only have the general and specific characteristics of the market been analyzed; so have the responses of competitive firms that are pursuing these markets.

For new firms in a market, the competitive analysis has another advantage. Because the other firms have already adjusted to market conditions with their own strategies, their own approaches to the market are suggestive of successful and unsuccessful ways to enter and compete in it. Their trials and errors should become a guide to avoiding mistakes already made and activities already proved unsuccessful, either by their nature or by the way they were carried out by existing firms.

Notes

1. Arthur A. Thompson and A.J. Strickland, *Strategic Management: Concepts and Cases* (Plano, Tex.: Business Publications, Inc., 1984), p. 152.

2. Michael E. Porter, "How Competitive Forces Shape Strategy," *Harvard Business Review* 57, No. 2 (March–April 1979):141.

3. Adapted from C.H. McGregor and Paul C. Chakmas, *Retail Management Problems*, 4th ed. (Homewood, Ill.: Richard D. Irwin, 1970), pp. 255–256.

4. Stewart H. Rewaldt, James. R. Scott, and Martin R. Warshaw, *Introduction to Marketing Management* (Homewood, Ill.: Richard D. Irwin, 1977), p. 85.

5. Wroe Alderson, *Dynamic Marketing Behavior* (Homewood, Ill.: Richard D. Irwin, 1965), Chapter 8.

6. The section is based on Philip Kotler, *Marketing Management: Analysis, Planning, and Control*, 4th ed. (Englewood Cliffs, N.J.: Prentice-Hall, 1980), Chapter 11.

Part III
Financial Analysis

5
Revenue and Cost Analysis

After the external analysis has been completed, the next step in market opportunity analysis is the financial analysis of opportunities. Regardless of the decision-making situation involved, the financial analysis should contain at least three different types of analysis: (1) revenue analysis, (2) costs analysis, and (3) analysis of return on investment (ROI).

One of the most beneficial ways to combine these three types of analysis is to embrace the concept of a pro forma income statement as the basic document to be generated by the financial analysis. A pro forma income statement is a projected income statement for a specific future time period using estimates of revenues and costs associated with that time period. It provides an estimate of cash flows to be produced by a given opportunity, which can be discounted to determine the present value of these cash flows. This, in turn, is used in calculating the rate of return anticipated achievable from a given opportunity.

A pro forma income statement for a proposed opportunity is shown in table 5-1. The approach used for this opportunity was to develop three alternative pro formas, each based on a different assumption about revenues generated by the new venture. This permits identifying the most optimistic, most pessimistic, and the most likely outcome. It is also in line with a more realistic approach to demand forecasting, which produces a range of sales volume for new projects. When products or services have already been on the market for several years, industry sales history is available to use in projecting sales.

Revenues and costs change over the course of a product's life cycle. High investments in promotion and building distribution produce losses in early years; on the other hand, reduced variable costs achieved by increasing production efficiency and technological improvement may produce high profit levels in later years.

Since the financial analysis is usually long run in nature, either the pro forma must be estimated for each year for some assumed length of time or an average year that is three to five years into the future can be used. Then the discounted cash flows from this year are used as an average for the venture's anticipated life to calculate the ROI or break-even point.

Table 5–1
Pro Forma Income Statement

	Low (Pessimistic)	Medium (Most Likely)	High (Optimistic)
Sales	$3,500,000	$4,500,000	$5,500,000
Cost of sales	2,500,000	3,400,000	4,300,000
Gross margin	$1,000,000	$1,100,000	$1,200,000
Expenses			
Direct selling	457,000	480,000	512,000
Advertising	157,000	168,000	180,000
Transportation and storage	28,000	38,000	48,000
Depreciation	15,000	15,000	15,000
Credit and collections	12,000	14,000	16,000
Financial and clerical	29,000	38,000	47,000
Administrative	55,000	55,000	55,000
Total expenses	$ 753,000	$ 808,000	$ 873,000
Profit before taxes	$ 247,000	$ 292,000	$ 327,000
Net profit after taxes	$ 128,440	$ 151,840	$ 170,040
Cash flow	$ 143,440	$ 166,840	$ 185,040

If subjective probabilities are assigned to each alternative, then decision tree analysis can be used to calculate an expected value for the cash flow from the project. Otherwise, the ROI can be calculated for each alternative and compared with a predetermined rate to evaluate the financial impact.

Developing a pro forma income statement requires a forecast of both expected revenues and operating expenses. The procedures for developing these estimates are discussed in this chapter.

Thus the revenue analysis produces an estimate of revenues, the costs analysis produces an estimate of the costs associated with those revenues, and the analysis of ROI or break-even point relates those returns to the investment to be made in the decision. This, in turn, provides the answer to the basic question posed in financial analysis: "What is the projected financial impact of pursuing this opportunity?"

Nonprofit Financial Analysis

Many nonprofit organizations fail to apply this basic approach to their decision making. A large hospital, for example, decided to build a new wing for geriatric outpatients to provide rehabilitation services for patients suffering from major traumas such as strokes or heart attacks. The facility was built to accommodate 100 patients, but when it opened, only 2 patients showed up to take advantage of the new facility. An analysis of demand for such services prior to their provision would have avoided such a costly mistake.

Although the analysis of returns from a decision made by a nonprofit organization uses different criteria, such an evaluation should be done nonetheless. This type of analysis is simply an application of a basic management concept: evaluate the impact of a decision *before* you make it. This principle applies to nonprofit as well as profit-oriented institutions.

Forecasting Market Share

Once the size of the total market has been estimated and the competition analyzed, the next step is to estimate the sales revenue the opportunity can be expected to generate on an annual basis. The point is not trying to determine how many consumers will buy a product or service but, rather, how many will buy *your* offering.

For established markets, this involves estimating market share. The question is: "What share of total sales can we reasonably expect to attain?" The percentage is then converted to a dollar amount—the sales revenue expected in a given time period. The key element in the estimate at this point is judgment. (If a test market is used later in the development process, this estimate can be reevaluated for soundness.)

This judgment is based on an analysis of your offering versus competitive offerings. If four competitors are in the market and your product is expected to compete on an equal footing with other offerings, then a 20 percent market share should be used as an initial estimate. This basic estimate would then be raised or lowered to reflect competitive strengths and weaknesses in the market.

For new products and services not currently on the market, an acceptance rate must be estimated. The acceptance rate is the proportion of the segment that will buy your product or use your service. Two approaches can be used to estimate the acceptance rate. These are described below.

Judgment Estimates

One way to estimate the acceptance rate is to use judgment. After careful analysis of the market, the person preparing the feasibility study sets the rate, in conjunction with other people who are knowledgeable about the market. Such an educated guess can be effective if people who know about a market—retailers, wholesalers, industrial users—are consulted. This estimate also reflects what the company can bring to the market in terms of marketing skills, innovation, and the life.

Consumer Surveys

Another approach to estimating the proportion of consumers who would buy a new offering is to conduct a survey of consumers. Data obtained in this way have been referred to as "iffy": "I would buy your product *if* it were offered on the market, and *if* I was in the market at that time, and *if* . . ." For industrial users, however, surveys can be effective since industrial firms are in a position to evaluate the use of a product more judiciously than many individual consumers.

These two approaches are often combined to provide a sales forecast. A set of assumptions—about market acceptance, competitive reactions, economic conditions, and so forth—must also be developed as a basis for the forecast. These assumptions must precede the actual dollar forecast used in the pro forma income statement.

An example of how these approaches can be combined to estimate sales revenue is shown in table 5–2. This exhibit shows the estimates of attendance at a proposed water recreation center. Assumptions were made about the penetration or acceptance rates by market segment and repeat visits.

Table 5–2
Attendance Projections

Facts/Assumptions	Attendance: Alternative 1986 Forecasts		
	Low	Most Likely	High
Attendance/penetration			
1. Local target market			
Population	520,000	520,000	520,000
Target market (Ages 10–25)	120,000	120,000	120,000
Penetration	.65	.70	.85
Attendance	78,000	84,000	102,000
2. Local market general population			
Population	110,000	110,000	110,000
Penetration	.03	.05	.07
Attendance	3,300	5,500	7,700
3. Regional market			
Population	100,000	100,000	100,000
Penetration	.10	.15	.20
Attendance	10,000	15,000	20,000
4. Tourist market			
Population	250,000	250,000	250,000
Penetration	.03	.05	.07
Attendance	7,500	12,500	17,500
5. Group sales market			
Attendance	18,000	20,500	25,000
6. Repeat business			
Attendance	72,000	78,000	95,000
Total attendance (sum of 1–6)	188,800	215,500	267,200

The admission charge was anticipated to be $5/person, giving the following alternative sales forecasts:

Low forecast	$ 944,000	(188,800 × $5)
Most likely	$1,077,500	(215,500 × $5)
High forecast	$1,336,000	(267,200 × $5)

A sales range of about $950,000–$1,340,000 was estimated. To derive a figure for the pro forma income statement, the following probabilities were assigned to each forecast:

Low forecast	.25
Most likely	.50
High forecast	.25

The expected sales revenue was then computed as follows:

$$E_{SR} = (\$944,000)\,(.25) + (\$1,077,500)\,(.50)$$
$$+ (\$1,336,000)\,(.25)$$
$$E_{SR} = \$1,108,750$$

This final value ($1,108,750) was used as the estimate of sales revenue to be generated from attendance sales in the pro forma income statement.

Cost Analysis

The bottom line at any operation or project is significantly affected by the underlying cost structure. Consequently, cost analysis is closely allied with revenue analysis. Once revenue estimates have been made, cost analysis must be carefully considered. This chapter will discuss various cost concepts, cost information sources, cost sensitivity analysis, technical analysis, and cost forecasting.

Cost Concepts

Accounting for the costs of conducting business operations is complex. This is also true of analyzing costs for market opportunity. As a business functions, assets lose their original identity. Business operations convert the assets into some other form. For example, raw materials of many kinds may go into a final manufactured product, and many of these raw materials may be unrecognizable in the end product. Costs, however, are traced through the business operations as the assets and resources are converted into goods and services. Since the profits and losses of a business are measured as the difference between the *revenue* received from customers and the *costs* associated with delivery of the products or services, a project cannot be judged as feasible or profitable without dependable cost estimates.

Types of Costs

Because there are many different types of costs, costs must be chosen carefully to match the purpose for which they are used. Care must be taken to understand the specific application of a cost under consideration.

Costs can be divided into several major categories, some of which will be instrumental in developing the project cost summary discussed later in the chapter.

Period Costs

Period costs are associated with and measured according to *time intervals* rather than goods or sources. For example, equipment rental may be at the rate of $1,200 a month. Regardless of the amount of business or product supported by the equipment, the rental cost of the equipment remains $1,200 each month. This expense amount is allocated against revenue according to the time interval, without regard to the amount of business transacted. Equipment expense for the year will show $14,400 on the income statement. Generally speaking, selling and administrative costs are designated as period costs.

Product Costs

Some costs are not appropriately classified as period costs. Some situations in the income determination process call for costs to be offset as expenses against the *activity, good,* or *service* that produced the revenue. Under this concept of income determination, the period in which the benefit is received is the period in which the costs should be expressed and deducted as expenses. Following our equipment rental example, the equipment rental for a certain period *should not* be charged off as rent expense for that period if the goods produced by the equipment are not sold until a later period. If costs of this type are handled as product costs, they are matched against the revenue generated from their sale in the period of that sale. In most cases, manufacturing costs are treated as product costs rather than period costs and are included in the cost of goods sold.

Fixed Costs

Costs that can be expected to remain constant over a period of time regardless of activity levels are called fixed costs. Fixed costs include executive salaries, interest charges, rent, insurance, equipment leases, depreciation, engineering and technical support, and product development expense. Obviously, a fixed cost, like any other cost, can be increased or decreased, particularly in an inflationary period. These variations, however, are caused by other external factors, not caused by the firm's output or activity.

Fixed costs can be subdivided as *committed fixed costs* and *discretionary fixed costs*. Management decisions may commit a company to conforming to a certain payment schedule for a number of years in the future. Costs incurred in this way are committed fixed costs. The costs related to acquiring a new building are examples of committed costs. On the other hand, discretionary fixed costs are established as part of a budget that can be altered by management action on a monthly, quarterly, or yearly basis. These costs are much more easily altered and highly flexible. Examples of discretionary fixed costs are the research and development budget or supervisory salaries that are set by management action.

Variable & Semivariable Costs

Costs that vary closely with production are considered variable costs. In the strictest sense of the term, variable costs should vary in direct proportion to changes in production levels. Direct material costs and direct labor costs are good examples of variable costs. Most costs, however, are *semivariable*. Semivariable costs tend to fluctuate with volume, but not in a direct relationship to production. Market research expense, advanced research expense, advertising and sales promotion expense, supplies expense, and maintenance expense are all examples of semivariable expenses. In some cases semivariable costs can be broken down into fixed and variable components to make application for decisionmaking possible.

Direct and Indirect Costs

Direct costs are those identifiable with a particular product, department, or activity. Indirect costs are not directly identifiable with any particular product, activity, or department. Often the distinction between direct and indirect costs depends on the unit under consideration. A cost of specific supplies used may be identified directly as a cost of a particular department but may not be a direct cost of the product manufactured. When a cost can be directly connected to the unit under consideration, it is considered a direct cost relative to that unit. When a cost is associated with a unit only through allocation, it is an indirect cost.

Controllable and Noncontrollable Costs

Like direct and indirect costs, a reference point is required to classify costs as controllable or noncontrollable. Obviously, at some point in the organizational structure all costs are controllable. Top management can dispose of property, eliminate personnel, terminate research projects, or do whatever else is necessary to control costs. At middle and lower levels of management, however, costs can be termed uncontrollable. If a specific level of management has the authority to authorize certain costs, then these costs are considered controllable at that level. A plant manager, for example, may have control over the supplies used by a plant but may have no control of promotional costs established by central headquarters.

Sunk Costs

A sunk cost is usually one that was spent in the past and is irrelevant to a decision under consideration. This concept will be discussed further in the next chapter in relation to the capital budgeting decision. Sunk costs may be either variable or fixed.

Differential Costs

The purpose of cost analysis is to provide management with the data necessary to compare alternatives and make choices. In order to simplify the comparison of alternatives, any costs that remain the same regardless of the alternative will be disregarded in the analysis. A difference in cost between one course of action and another is referred to as a differential cost. In most cases the decision will result in an increased cost. This increased differential cost is often referred to specifically as an *incremental cost*.

Differential costs are referred to as *marginal costs* when the differential cost is the additional cost required to produce one more unit of a product.

Opportunity Costs

Ordinarily, costs are viewed as outlays or expenditures that must be made to obtain goods and services. The concept of opportunity costs extends this to include sacrifices that are made by foregoing benefits or returns. An opportunity cost takes into consideration the fact that choosing one of several alternatives precludes receiving the benefits of the rejected alternatives. The sacrifice of a return from a rejected alternative is referred to as the opportunity cost of the chosen alternative.

Many of the costs mentioned here are overlapping. Thus fixed cost may also be a sunk cost, an uncontrollable cost, or a period cost. Judgment must be used in identifying specific costs in the development of cost estimates for a specific opportunity.

Data Sources

Many sources of data are found in a company's historical records. These records can provide cost information to establish reasonable cost estimates. Many other sources of data also provide information that forms the basis of a reliable cost forecast:

Trade publications: These provide comparative financial ratios, information on cost of goods sold, gross margin data, and other information.

Time studies: These establish standards for estimating labor cost.

Experiments: These test processes in terms of time, material, labor, and other resources necessary to complete production.

Pilot plant or process activities: These involve the intermittent or continuous operation of a new plant activity or process to perfect engineering specifications and to establish cost standards.

Historical cost data: This can include past material cost, labor cost, overhead expense, administrative costs, utility expense, and many other categories of expense.

Interviews: These include personal interviews, telephone interviews, and mail interviews designed to gather data that provide primary cost information unavailable from other sources.

Other sources:

Wholesale Prices and Price Indexes. Washington, D.C.: U.S. Bureau of Labor Statistics. This report periodically provides statistical representation of various prices.

Standard & Poor's Industry Surveys. New York: McGraw-Hill. These surveys provide overall statistical data and outlook for various industries.

Standard & Poor's: S&P also provides special in-depth coverage in reports on specific areas—the recreation industry, the entertainment industry, and so forth.

Agricultural Statistics, U.S. Department of Agriculture. Washington, D.C.: U.S. Government Printing Office. This resource includes statistical data concerning prices and supply of agriculturally related items.

Various *census reports* are available for various types of activities—construction, wholesale trade, housing manufacturing, and transportation.

Department of Commerce: The regional offices of the Department of Commerce have resource libraries and extensive stores that provide a large amount of resource information for forecasting purposes.

Business Periodical Index. New York: H.W. Wilson Company. Most major libraries have available this resource index to periodicals with an author-subject approach to areas of business interest.

Thomas Register. New York: Thomas Publishing Company. This series includes products and services, company addresses, and company personnel.

Survey of Buying Power. New York: Sales Management. Data such as population figures, income figures, and retail sales figures are provided for specific areas of the country.

See appendix A, "Sources of Published Data," for further sources of information.

Cost Behavior, Sensitivity Analysis, and Risk Analysis

Before moving on to the actual development of detailed cost forecasts, a discussion of sensitivity analysis is in order. *Sensitivity analysis* is a technique that illustrates how the costs of an operation or activity will be affected by changes in variables or by errors in the input data. Sensitivity analysis is sometimes called "what if" analysis, because it asks and answers questions such as "What if labor cost increases an average of $1.75/hour?" or "What if sales fall to 350,000 units?" The starting point for sensitivity analysis is to establish a *base case* or *most likely* situation. Once the base case or most likely forecast elements are established for items such as unit sales, sale price, fixed costs, and variable costs, the analyst can selectively change key variables to determine their impact on the base case results. The analyst can ask all the "what if" questions necessary to see the effect of changes in variables such as product price, raw material costs, and operating costs on the overall results of a project. The analyst can determine which variable has the most negative or positive effect on the project's profitability. Given the possible range of a variable, such as material cost, the range of effects on the outcome can be calculated and charted. The more sensitive the outcome is to the tested variable, the more serious an error in estimating the variable would be. The purpose of sensitivity analysis is to identify the variables that have the stronger impact on the outcome of a project. Sensitivity analysis is effective in determining the consequences of a change in a variable.

Sensitivity Analysis: An Example

The following example shows sensitivity analysis as illustrated by break-even analysis. Although break-even analysis has its limitations, it is a useful analytical technique for studying the relationships among fixed costs, variable costs, and revenue. The relationship between costs and revenues must be analyzed to determine at what level of sales total costs are covered by total revenues. Break-even analysis indicates the point at which there is no profit and no loss. The break-even point serves as a base indication of how many units of product must be sold if a company is to avoid a loss. Figure 5–1 illustrates the break-even concept.

In order to construct a break-even analysis, one must have estimates of fixed costs, variable costs per unit, volume of production, and price per unit. As discussed earlier, fixed costs do not change with the level of production. Variable costs are directly related to units of production and change with the level of production. Table 5–3 illustrates different costs attributable to fixed costs and variable costs.

Where:

$$FC = \text{Fixed costs}$$
$$P = \text{Sales price per unit}$$
$$Q = \text{Quantity of production in units}$$
$$V = \text{Variable cost per unit}$$
$$P - V = \text{Contribution margin}$$

$$\text{Break-even point} = \frac{\text{Fixed costs}}{\text{Contribution margin}} = \frac{FC}{P - V}$$

Expressed another way:

Total revenue = Total cost at the break-even point: $TR = TC$

or:

$$TR - TC = 0 \text{ (at the break-even point)}$$
$$TR = PQ = \text{Total revenue}$$
$$TC = FC + VQ = \text{Total cost}$$

Substituting:

$PQ = FC + VQ$ Solving for Q will derive break-even quantity.

In a situation where a new production line is being considered, the following data might be indicated by market analysis:

Production line capacity = 2,200 units

P = potential selling price = $220/unit

$ Revenue

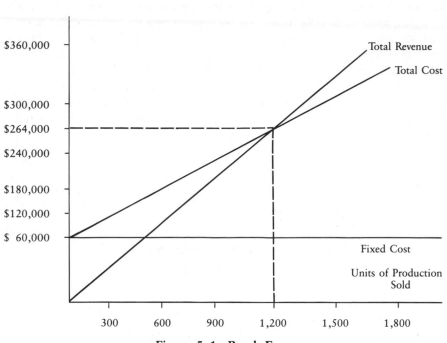

Figure 5–1. Break-Even

FC = fixed costs = $60,000

V = variable costs = $170/unit

Figure 5–1 graphically represents the break-even concept.
The point at which TR = FC, the break-even point, is 1,200 units.

$$\begin{aligned}
PQ &= FC + V{\cdot}Q \\
\$220(Q) &= \$60,000 + \$170(Q) \\
\$220(Q) - \$170(Q) &= \$60,000 \\
\$50(Q) &= \$60,000 \\
(Q) &= 1,200 \text{ units}
\end{aligned}$$

Solved another way:

$$\begin{aligned}
\text{Break-even point by quantity} &= \frac{FC}{P - V} \\
&= \frac{\$60,000}{\$220 - \$170} \\
&= \frac{\$60,000}{\$50} \\
&= 1,200
\end{aligned}$$

Table 5–3
Cost Categories

Fixed Costs	Variable Costs
Depreciation	Factory labor
Plant utilities	Material costs
Fixed utilities	Commissions
Office expense	Freight in and out
Insurance	Variable factory expense
Rentals	Utilities (other than fixed)
Debt interest	Cost of goods sold
Salaries (executive and office)	Sales expense

With a selling price of $220 per unit, the break-even point is illustrated by the intersection at the lines representing total revenue and total costs in figure 5–1. To apply sensitivity analysis, the analyst might put in various values of volume, price, variable cost, and fixed cost to measure their relative effect on profit.

Table 5–4 illustrates changes in volume of production of 100 unit increments above and below the break-even point. The table also shows the impact of these changes in production on profits. The table shows that changes in the volume of production near the break-even point result in large variations in profits and losses. Using the same basic formula just shown, an analyst can test the sensitivity of price and profits (see table 5–5.) Since our example shows a production capacity of 2,200 units and a break-even point of 1,200 units, if market analysis shows a market potential in the range of 1,400–1,700 units, then the project can be considered a viable proposition. Further calculations can be made to estimate a range of profits based on our previous cost assumptions.

$$\text{Profit} = \$220\,(1,700) - \$60,000 - \$170\,(1,700)$$
$$\text{Profit} = \$374,000 - \$60,000 - \$289,000$$
$$\text{Profit} = 25,000$$

$$\text{Profit} = \$220\,(1,400) - \$60,000 - \$170\,(1,400)$$
$$\text{Profit} = \$308,000 - \$60,000 - \$238,000$$
$$\text{Profit} = \$10,000$$

This same information is given in table 5–4.

The analyst can use the same calculation method to compute a minimum sales price for any level of volume. Other variations can be used to determine the effect of changes on profit and loss. Break-even analysis, used in this way, provides managers with a profit or loss estimate at different levels of sales and at different cost estimates. It can also approximate the effect of a change in selling prices on the company.

Table 5–4
Sensitivity Analysis of Production and Profits

Volume	Profit	Percentage Change
700	($25,000)	25%
800	(20,000)	33.3%
900	(15,000)	50%
1,000	(10,000)	100%
1,100	(5,000)	
1,200	-0-	
1,300	5,000	
1,400	10,000	100%
1,500	15,000	50%
1,600	20,000	33.3%
1,700	25,000	25%

Sensitivity analysis can be applied to other techniques of analysis as well. It may be used in the capital budgeting decision using discounted cash flows. Changes in the required rate of return can be quickly converted into changes in the project's net present value, which represents the potential increase in wealth the project offers. The discounted cash flow method of making capital budgeting decisions will be discussed more fully in chapter 6.

Other uses of sensitivity analysis include testing price change impact on sales plans, testing changes in the productive life of equipment, and testing the effect of changes in demand on profitability.

Risk Analysis

Sensitivity analysis is appropriate for asking "what if" questions and for determining the consequences of various changes in variables. Sensitivity analysis, however, cannot identify the likelihood that a change in a variable will occur. Risk analysis is the process used to identify and assign a degree of likelihood

Table 5–5
Sensitivity Analysis of Price and Profits
Volume set at 1,200 units)

Price	Profit	Percentage Change
180	(48,000)	33.3%
190	(36,000)	50%
200	(24,000)	100%
210	(12,000)	
220	-0-	
230	12,000	
240	24,000	100%
250	16,000	50%
260	48,000	33.3%

to changes in important variables that may be essential in determining the feasibility of a project. This will be discussed in greater detail in chapter 6.

The Process of Cost Forecasting. The use of cost estimates for planning purposes is very important in developing the project cost summary. The firm's chief accounting officer should be instrumental in assembling the cost data used as a basis for a firm's activities

As demand analysis estimated the market potential of the new project, product, or services, cost analysis is the basis for determining the actual financial and technical feasibility of the proposed activity.

Cost estimates must be provided for the following categories:

1. Fixed investments such as land, buildings, fixtures, and other equipment
2. Manufacturing costs such as direct material cost, direct labor cost, and manufacturing overhead
3. Start-up expense such as training costs, increased overtime, scrap expense, consulting fees, and legal fees
4. Other related expenses.

A broad series of assumptions and decisions must be made to provide the framework for developing these cost estimates. A detailed step-by-step forecasting checklist must be followed to establish accurate cost estimates. This checklist is illustrated in table 5–6.

Table 5–6
Cost Forecast Checklist

	Yes	No
1. Are the objectives of the study clearly defined?	_____	_____
2. Are the various alternatives clearly identified?	_____	_____
3. Are reliable cost estimates available for fixed investment, manufacturing costs, and other related start-up costs?	_____	_____
4. Are the likely changes in material costs identified?	_____	_____
5. Are the likely changes in labor costs identified?	_____	_____
6. Are the changes in unit factory overhead rates caused by the proposed production identified?	_____	_____
7. Has the demand analysis provided a realistic forecast of sales?	_____	_____
8. Have the production personnel provided estimated overhead costs for the new project based on the sales forecast?	_____	_____
9. Have all appropriate departments input their budget estimates (general and administrative departments, warehousing and distribution, selling and advertising, research and development, and so on)?	_____	_____
10. Has a final project cost summary been completed?	_____	_____

Accurate cost estimates require a solid analysis of a project's technical requirements. Projects will vary in the depth of this type of analysis. The technological complexity of the project, the amount of resources required to accomplish the project, and the number of viable alternatives will all influence the amount of attention given to the technical analysis. Most new ventures have enough unknown characteristics to necessitate close attention to the specific aspects of the project in order to achieve good cost estimates.

Technical Analysis. A large error in the technical study of a project can have a significant impact. An inadequate technical study can lead to an immediate failure of the new venture or to costly readjustment of project goals. Estimates of manufacturing costs, investment requirements, start-up costs, and other related expenses necessitate an accurate technical study.

The technical study should include the following seven steps:

1. *Will the process work? Can the product be produced? Can the service be delivered?*

In some cases, experiments, research, or tests are required to determine if a new product or process is workable.

2. *Are proper inventory estimates made?*

Proper inventory levels are necessary to meet demand requirements and to maintain an even production schedule. The necessary inventory level must be known in order to make the appropriate cost estimates for inventory requirements. Manufacturing firms usually have three types of inventory:

1. *Raw Materials:* Raw materials and component parts are influenced by production schedules, anticipated sales, reliability of supply sources, quantity discounts, and price volatility.

2. *Work-in-process:* This type of inventory consists of the partially completed products located in the plant. The level of work-in-process inventory is affected by the characteristics of the production process, particularly its length. This type of inventory is necessary for a smooth production schedule.

3. *Finished goods:* The level of finished products in stock depends on the right balance between production and sales. A safety stock is necessary to ensure that there is no delay in filling customer orders. Also, finished goods will build up when sales fluctuate and levels of production do not. Inventories of this type are used for production stabilization purposes.

Inventory levels should be estimated to minimize the total cost of ordering inventory and holding inventory. Estimating inventories at approximately 10 percent of the forecasted annual demand provided by the market analysis is a good rule of thumb.

3. Has the production schedule been developed?

The projected production requirements are required to establish a production schedule. The market analysis should provide estimates of monthly or quarterly sales that can be used for this purpose. After a production schedule has been developed, tangible production cost estimates can be made and prepared for the project cost summary. The cost of the production process must include all the sequence of operations and functions required to convert raw material inventory into finished goods inventory. This should include the cost of:

Production equipment

Handling equipment (conveyors, hoists, cranes, and so forth)

Space requirements

Inventory levels

Personnel (production and supervision)

Delivery

Inspection

Maintenance

Step 3 leads, of necessity, directly into steps 4, 5, and 6

4. Are special tools and equipment necessary?

If the answer is yes, steps must be taken to analyze the costs related to these necessary items. Cost information concerning special tools and equipment can be obtained from equipment manufacturers, trade literature, other manufacturers using the same or similar equipment, or trade associations.

In some cases a capital budgeting analysis of equipment alternatives is necessary. Since present costs cannot be compared dollar for dollar with future costs, an equivalent annual cost in present-value terms should be used to choose among alternatives. The present-value method of discounting future cost amounts will be discussed and illustrated in chapter 6.

5. Have labor requirements and costs been established?

Accurate cost estimates require knowledge of how many employees are needed and the rates at which employees at various skill levels must be paid. This information can be used to determine final labor costs. Total workload requirements are estimated for each skill level. These totals are then multiplied by the appropriate pay rate for that level. In addition to direct production labor, factory overhead must be included. This category includes such things as maintenance, inspection, supervision, receiving, packing, shipping, control, analysis, safety, and quality control.

6. *Have the various space requirements and costs been established?*

Most projects will require various types of space considerations. Most common are production space, sales space, administrative space, and space for other services.

Production space includes work areas, storage areas, and testing areas. Layout charts and process charts can be helpful in calculating the actual square footage of space required.

Other space requirements should be reasonably estimated in order to calculate building or rental costs. These other areas include administrative offices, meeting rooms, sales areas, training rooms, accounting and auditing areas, a safety office, a security office, break rooms, a research and development area, a purchasing area, a quality control area, engineering, maintenance, warehouse space, a toolroom, and personnel offices.

If the project requires that a new building be constructed, then that aspect of the project should be approached as a feasibility project within the larger project. The same basic steps should be followed in examining market factors, cost factors, and financial considerations.

7. *Has the project cost summary been completed?*

The cost estimates obtained through the other steps in this process are important in defining the financial nature of an opportunity. The integrity of the financial analysis and the estimated return on investment depends on the accuracy of the demand analysis (sales estimates) and the cost analysis (cost estimates). These analyses should provide the parameters to determine ROI.

The project cost summary must include the basic cost elements mentioned at the beginning of the forecasting portion of this chapter: (1) fixed investment, (2) manufacturing cost, (3) start-up costs, and (4) other related costs. Table 5–7 illustrates a project cost summary that includes the four basic cost elements.

The project cost summary provides the information necessary for a projected statement of the cost of goods sold. This, coupled with information from the market analysis, provides the basis for the pro forma income statement, which estimates the profitability of the project. Pro forma income statements are exhibited on p. 000 of Appendix B. Additional aid can now be produced to aid the planner such as pro forma balance sheets, cash flow projections, and detailed cost summaries.

Forecasting Procedures

Cost forecasting can use many of the tools described in chatper 2 in relation to forecasting sales. Developing cost forecasts of totally new ventures for which

Table 5–7
Project Cost Summary

Category	Quantity	Description	Costs Monthly	Annual
Fixed investment				
		Land		
		Construction cost		
		Building cost		
		Security systems		
		Fire prevention systems		
		Furniture		
		Fixtures		
		Production equipment		
		Office equipment		
		Trucks		
Manufacturing costs				
		Direct material		
		Direct labor		
		Factory overhead		
		Maintenance		
		Utilities		
		Quality control		
		Office supplies		
		Rent		
		Insurance		
		Telephone		
		Depreciation		
		Taxes		
		Supervision		
		Toolroom		
		Miscellaneous expenses		
Start-up Costs				
		Financing expense		
		Consultants' fees		
		Training		
		Waste		
		Delay expense		
		Travel		
		Legal fees		
		Patents		
Other related requirements				
		Working capital requirements		
		Extraordinary expenses		
		Administrative expense		
		Salaries		
		Insurance		
		Supplies		
		Total cost		

there are no historical cost figures is more difficult and subject to greater error than forecasting for projects that have cost histories.

The correct procedure for forecasting costs varies from project to project. The objective of cost forecasting is to approximate the real expenses involved in an undertaking so that profitability can be projected. The actual procedure for forecasting cost may be determined by examining the objectives and resources of the principal to the venture.

The following forecasting techniques can be used to estimate costs:

1. *Judgment techniques:* Past experiences of key personnel have led to rules of thumb that in some cases can determine certain kinds of costs . These subjective techniques should not be the sole basis for cost analysis.

2. *Survey techniques:* Like market information, cost information can be acquired through consumer surveys. Personal or telephone interviews with persons experienced in the appropriate field are common. Such surveys of expert opinion can generate helpful cost data.

3. *Historical data techniques:* When historical data are available, cost forecasting can be accomplished by making certain subjective assumptions and then projecting historical cost elements into the future.

a. *Trend analysis:* Many hand calculators are programmed or programable to project costs at past points onto specific future dates. Plotting the

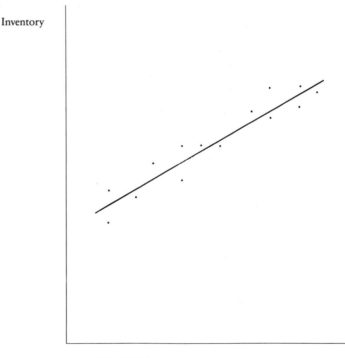

Figure 5–2. Scatter Diagram

past cost history of a certain element can be helpful. Scatter diagrams chart cost data for a number of periods (see figure 5–2). A line drawn midway between the high and low points is called the *line of best fit or the regression line.* Remember that many costs are distinct entities and cannot be projected in the same way sales can.

b. *Multiple regression:* Multiple regression is a more sophisticated approach to forecasting. In simple regression, a cost is assumed to be the function of only one variable. In multiple regression, however, the cost or dependent variable is associated with a number of variables.

4. *Percentage of sales:* Many costs can be adequately expressed in a percentage-of-sales format. Sales commissions, for example, are calculated as a percentage of sales. A good sales forecast is an essential foundation for this method of estimating costs. The percentage-of-sales method implies a linear relationship between sales and the expense item being calculated. Not only can certain expense items be forecast as a percentage of sales, but balance sheet items and external financing requirements can be developed by this method as well.

Summary

Accurately estimating the financial impact of a decision is extremely difficult. There are many unknowns and contingencies that cause forecasts to vary from actual revenues. Nonetheless, the revenue forecast is a prerequisite to complete financial analysis. Overly optimistic forecasts produce unrealistic expectations, whereas overly pessimistic predictions may lead a firm to pass up a good opportunity.

Accurate cost estimates are extremely important in opportunity assessment also. Cost overruns are common and often disastrous to the principal involved in a venture. Consequently, every attempt should be made to *identify* and *estimate* accurately all costs associated with a specific opportunity. This is best accomplished by a thorough technical study and an accompanying cost forecast. The results of forecasting should yield a project cost summary that can be used in determining return on investment, the subject of the next chapter.

6
Profitability Analysis

T he final and perhaps the overriding consideration in defining the exact nature of an opportunity is the potential profitability it represents. Previous chapters have dealt with the analysis of demand and the forecasting of costs. This chapter will focus on the analytical techniques that can be used to ensure profitable investment decisions.

One of the major objectives of all the time, energy, and resources marshaled toward a project is to generate a good profit. What represents a "good" profit, however, may be a matter of personal judgment. It is advisable to establish acceptable levels of ROI before choosing project alternatives.

Return on Investment

Simply stated, return on investment (ROI) is how much an investment returns to you on an annual basis. ROI is the most meaningful and popular measure of economic success. It is a term that is widely understood by accountants, financial analysts, bankers, managers, and investors. ROI analysis is very helpful in determining the health of a project. ROI itself, however, does not measure the safety of an investment—only its performance expressed as a percentage.

ROI can be calculated by dividing net profit by the total investment required to generate the profit:

$$\text{Return on investment (ROI)} = \frac{\text{Net Profit}}{\text{Total investment}}$$

$$\text{ROI} = 21.5\% = \frac{\$\ 42,000}{\$195,000}$$

ROI can be calculated for a wide range of investments, including savings accounts, profit centers, divisions, and entire companies.

ROI can also be expressed as a combination of the profit margin on sales and the turnover activity ratio of an investment:

$$\frac{\text{Net profit}}{\text{Sales}} = \text{Profit Margin}$$

$$\frac{\text{Sales}}{\text{Investment}} = \text{Turnover of assets}$$

$$\frac{\text{Net profit}}{\text{Sales}} \times \frac{\text{Sales}}{\text{Investment}} = \text{ROI}$$

This second approach to ROI brings together the profitability margin on sales and the activity ratio of asset (investment) turnover. This approach takes into consideration the combination of the efficient use of assets (investments) and the profit margin on sales. This method, the duPont system of financial analysis, has been widely accepted in U.S. industry.

Financial Analysis

Financial analysis and capital budgeting consist of the process of selecting among alternative investments in land, buildings, productive equipment, and other assets for future gain. Since these decisions usually commit a firm to a long-term course of action, careful analysis is required to identify the potential return.

Capital budgeting is theoretically simple. You simply list all the investment opportunities available, rank them according to profitability, and accept all investments up to the point at which marginal benefits equal marginal cost. In reality, however, the complexity of revolving planning horizons makes the choice of capital outlays more difficult. Differences in project length, start-up time, and payout time make meaningful comparisons among investment alternatives problematic.

The depth of the economic analysis needed depends on the type of project, its urgency, and the firm's objectives. For example, a burned-out generator in a power plant must be replaced. The choice is not replacement versus non-replacement; the decision concerns only which particular generator is most productive, least expensive, or most readily available.

Before discussing in detail the analytical techniques for determining profitability and making capital decisions, a framework for the decision process—a *decision flow chart*—should be established.

Step 1   Define the problem.

Step 2   Identify alternatives.

Step 3   Identify relevant costs and revenues that will change because of
the action taken.

Step 4   Determine the alternative that has the most beneficial result.

Step 1: Problem Definition

This first step appears obvious, but it is often overlooked. A problem
statement—for example, "The problem is we need more trucks"—may not be
a problem statement at all but, rather, a suggested alternative solution. Too
often decision makers jump prematurely to step 2 without clearly articulating
the problem. The importance of proper problem definition cannot be overem-
phasized. Replacement of a worn-out piece of equipment, development of a
new product, and construction of a new plant all create uniquely complex problems. Each of these examples generally produces several alternatives, which
must be identified and evaluated clearly.

Step 2: Identify Alternatives

Alternative actions can range from doing nothing, to going out of business,
to replacing with the same type of equipment, replacing with different equipment, replacing with larger or smaller equipment, and so on. From this wide
range of alternatives, only the appropriate alternatives should be selected for
further analysis.

Step 3: Identify Relevant Costs and Revenues

The next step is to identify the costs and revenues that will change as a result
of the action taken. Chapter 3 dealt with many aspects of technical analysis
and cost forecasting that also apply to this step in capital budgeting. It is inappropriate to assume that past operating costs will apply to new ventures.
Although it is tempting simply to project historical cost into the future, it is
very hazardous. Methods of dealing with the uncertainty surrounding the cost
and revenue flows involved in capital budgeting must be incorporated to identify and estimate costs of revenues realistically. These methods will be discussed
later.

The basic question asked in step 3 is: "What changes in costs and revenues
will occur because of an action taken?" Other questions are:

"What additional revenues will be generated?"

"What revenues will be lost?"

"What is the *net* impact of the action on revenue?"

"What additional costs will be generated?"

"What costs will be eliminated?"

"What is the *net* impact of the action on costs?"

The preceding questions lead us to the economic principle of incremental changes in cash flow. The focus is on the economic cash flow concept. Once an after-tax cash flow change has been determined, we are ready for step 4.

Step 4: Determine the Alternative with the
Most Beneficial Result

The capital budgeting decision alternative with the most positive ROI is generally considered the superior one. The specific method of analysis used to calculate which alternative has the most sufficient economic returns over the life of the investment must in some way take into account the trade-off between current cash outlay and future cash inflow.

Methods of Analyzing Investments

There are many methods for evaluating investment alternatives prior to making the capital budgeting decision. Some of the more common methods will be discussed here.

The focus of capital budgeting is to make decisions that maximize the value of a firm's investment. You must choose a method that will answer most appropriately the question, "Which is the most profitable alternative?" The most common criteria for choosing among alternatives are non–time value methods and time value methods.

1. Non–time value methods
   a. Payback period
   b. Simple return on investment
   c. Average return on investment

2. Time value methods
   a. Net present value
   b. Internal rate of return
   c. Present-value index

Each of these methods has its advantages and disadvantages, which will be discussed along with the description of each method.

The Payback Period

The payback period is simply an estimate of how long it will take for the investment to pay for itself. No interest factors are included in the calculations. Once the payback period has been determined, it is usually compared with a rule of thumb or standard period. If the investment is predicted to pay for itself in less time than the standard period, the investment would be made. In deciding between mutually exclusive alternatives, the one with the shortest payback period is generally chosen.

The payback period can be calculated in several ways. The most common one uses the formula:

$$\text{Payback} = \frac{\text{Net investment outlay}}{\text{Net annual cash flow benefits}}$$

When annual cash flow benefits are irregular or investment outlay comes in various time frames, table 6–1 can be used to determine the payback period. In this case the payback period is four years. The payback period method is widely used because of its ease of calculation. Because it does not take into consideration the time value of money, however, it has serious flaws in its logic.

Advantages

1. The calculations are easy.
2. Choosing the project with the shortest payback period has the most favorable short-run effect on earnings per share.
3. The method is easily understood.

Table 6–1
Calculation of Payback Period

Year	Investment Outlay	Annual Cash Flow Benefits	Cumulative Cash Flow
1	$150,000	$40,000	($110,000)
2	10,000	40,000	(80,000)
3	-0-	40,000	(40,000)
4	-0-	40,000	-0-
5	-0-	40,000	40,000
6	-0-	20,000	60,000
7	-0-	20,000	80,000

Disadvantages

1. The method completely ignores all cash flows beyond the payback period.
2. It does not adjust for risk related to uncertainty.
3. It ignores the time value of money.

Some firms are beginning to use the payback method in combination with one or more of the time value methods described next. When this is done, the payback method is used as a risk measurement, and the time value method as an indicator of profitability.

Simple ROI

Simple ROI method is an outgrowth of the logic of the payback method. This method can be represented by manipulating the payback formula. It is an attempt to express the desirability of an investment in terms of percentage return on the original investment outlay:

$$ROI = \frac{\text{Net annual cash flow benefits}}{\text{Net investment outlay}}$$

The simple ROI method has all the drawbacks of the payback method. No reference is made to the project's economic life. An investment of $40,000 with an average annual benefit of $8,000 with yield a 20 percent return regardless of whether the length of the project is one, five, or ten years.

$$ROI = \frac{\$\ 8,000}{\$40,000}$$

Average ROI

The expected average rate of return is a measure of the estimated profitability of an investment. This calculation differs from simple ROI by employing the average net investment:

$$\text{Average ROI} = \frac{\text{Net annual cash flow benefits}}{\text{Average net investment outlay}}$$

Assuming straight-line depreciation and no residual value at the end of its life, an average investment would be equal to one-half of the original investment. Using the foregoing example, a net annual cash flow of $8,000 on an original expenditure of $40,000 would be 40 percent, not 20 percent:

$$\text{Average ROI} = \frac{\$8,000}{\$20,000} = 40\%$$

Advanced Concepts of Analysis: Time Value Methods

Investment decision values involve the trade-off between current dollar outlays and future benefits over a period of time. As a result, it is not prudent to ignore the timing of the benefits of investment alternatives. The quicker the return, the better. Money has value directly related to the timing of its receipt or disbursement. Delay in receiving money represents an opportunity cost in terms of lost income. Thus it is obviously preferable to receive benefits quickly and defer expenditures.

The Net-Present-Value Method

The basic idea of the net-present-value (NPV) method is to overcome the disadvantage of non–time value methods. The NPV method provides a balance of the trade-off between investment outlays and future benefits in terms of time-adjusted dollars. The present value of discounted cash flows is an amount at present that is equivalent to a project's cash flow for a particular interest rate. Generally, the interest rate used to discount future cash flows is a company's cost of capital rate. The NPV method involves:

1. Determining the present value of the net investment cost outlay
2. Estimating the future cash flow benefits
3. Discounting the future cash flows to present value at the appropriate cost of capital
4. Subtracting the present value of the costs from the present value of the benefits.

If the amount derived in step 4 is positive, then the investment is considered to be profitable since the time-adjusted internal rate of return on the investment is greater than the cost of capital. Conversely, a negative figure indicates that the project is earning a rate of return less than the cost of capital chosen by the firm as a standard of decision.

NPV can be calculated by the following formula:

$$\text{NPV} = \frac{R_1}{(1 + i)^1} + \frac{R_2}{(1 + i)^2} + \cdots + \frac{R_n}{(1 + i)^n} - \text{IC}$$

where:

$\quad$ NPV $\quad$ = net present value of the investment

$\quad$ R $\qquad$ = expected dollar returns or cash flows each year

$\quad$ i $\qquad$ = appropriate interest rate (cost of capital)

$\quad$ IC $\qquad$ = present value of the investment cost

$\quad$ n $\qquad$ = expected life of the project

The net present values of two alternative projects are illustrated in table 6–2. The project with the highest rate of return is project 1, even though the payback period is identical. The greatest benefit will be provided by selecting alternative 1. If the two projects are not mutually exclusive and funds are available, both investment opportunities should be accepted.

The present value method has several advantages that make it more suitable than the payback methods as a basis of comparing investments.

Advantages

1. It considers the time value of money.
2. It concentrates the values of costs and benefits in a comparable time frame.
3. It is fairly simple to understand and calculate.

Disadvantages

1. It assumes benefits and costs can be estimated for the lifetime of the project.
2. It requires equal time periods for comparison of several investment alternatives.
3. It is sensitive to changes in the interest rate used to discount the values.

Table 6–2
Net Present Values for Two Alternative Projects

Year	Net Return or Cash Flow		Interest Factor $(1 + i)^n$	PV of Cash Flow	
Project 1					
1	$ 400	×	0.91	$ 364	
2	500	×	0.83	415	
3	600	×	0.75	450	
4	800	×	0.68	544	
				1,773	PV of inflows
				− 1,500	less PV of cost
				$ 273	Net present value
Project 2					
1	$ 800	×	0.91	$ 728	
2	300	×	0.83	249	
3	400	×	0.75	300	
4	400	×	0.68	272	
				1,549	PV of inflows
				− 1,500	less PV of cost
				$ 49	Net present value

Internal Rate of Return (IRR)

The internal rate of return is simply the yield of a project. The IRR is defined as the interest rate that discounts the future cash flows, or receipts, and makes them equal to the initial cost outlay. The time value of money is taken into consideration. The formula used for NPV can also be used for IRR, with one slight variation. Instead of solving for NPV, the present value of the cost is made equal to the present value of the benefits. The equation is solved for the interest rate that will make the present value of the costs equal to the present value of the benefits. In other words, the internal rate of return of a project is the discount interest rate that generates an NPV of zero. The following is the NPV formula and the change necessary to create the IRR formula.

NPV formula

$$\text{NPV} = \frac{R_1}{(1 + i)^1} + \frac{R_2}{(1 + i)^2} + \ldots + \frac{R_n}{(1 + i)^n} - \text{IC}$$

IRR formula

$$\frac{R_1}{(1 + i)^1} + \frac{R_2}{(1 + i)^2} + \ldots + \frac{R_n}{(1 + i)^n} \quad \text{IC}$$

or

$$0 = \frac{R_1}{(1 + i)^1} + \frac{R_2}{(1 + i)^2} + \ldots + \frac{R_n}{(1 + i)^n} - \text{IC}$$

Solve for i and i = IRR.

In the new formula for IRR, i represents the interest rate that equates the present values of the benefits and the costs of a project. In the NPV formula, i represents the firm's cost of capital. When the cost of capital is used in the formula and NPV = 0, then the IRR is equal to the cost of capital. When NPV is positive, the IRR is greater than the cost of capital. When NPV is negative, the IRR is less than the cost of capital. Whenever the IRR is greater than the firm's cost of capital, the investment is a positive one. The IRR can be found by trial and error. The IRR method is widely accepted as a ranking device. The yield is reasonably accurate and much superior to that of the simple payback or simple ROI method.

Advantages

1. Because the IRR method is closely related to the NPV method, it is familiar to many business practitioners and thus more readily accepted.

2. Calculation of the firm's cost of capital is *not* required as it is with the NPV method.

3. The method time-values money.

Disadvantages

1. The IRR method does not do a good job of comparing investments that differ greatly in magnitude. For example, a $20,000 investment with an IRR of 42 percent cannot be compared with an investment of $100,000 with an IRR of 30 percent. It may be far better to marshal all resources toward the $100,000 investment, even though the IRR is lower than for the other investment.

2. Similarly, the length of life of the investment is also important. It may be more advantageous to invest funds at a lower IRR for a longer term than to invest for a short term for a slightly higher IRR. The pertinent criticism of the IRR method is that it assumes reinvestment can be made at the IRR, which may not be true.

Present-Value Index

This method is similar to the present-value method. A ratio is determined between the present value of the cash flow benefits and the present values of the net investment outlays. The *present-value index* is sometimes referred to as the benefit/cost ratio of discounted cash flows. Several alternative projects may have similar NPVs but require widely different investment amounts. To choose an alternative simply on the basis of size of NPV would ignore the relative different sizes of the projects. Equal NPVs coming from investments of different sizes will have different IRRs. A formal way of expressing this difference is to compare the projects on a benefit/cost basis.

$$\text{Present-value index} = \frac{\text{Present value of cash flow benefits}}{\text{Present value of net investment outlay}}$$

The higher the index, the better the project. Any present-value index over 1.0 exceeds the minimum standard built into the calculation of present value and should be funded. (Most projects, however, are competing for limited funds.) Table 6–3 gives examples of the present-value index.

Table 6–3 illustrates a comparison of the present-value index and the NPV ranking methods. Slightly different results are given. Notice that alternatives 1 and 3 have the same NPV, but alternative 1 has the higher present-value index and is therefore more favorable.

The advantages and disadvantages of the present-value index method are similar to those listed for the net-present-value method.

Table 6–3
Present-Value Index

Alternative	Present Value of Benefits	Present Value of Costs	Net Present Value	PV Index
1	$10,500	$ 8,500	$ 2,000	1.24
2	16,000	13,000	3,000	1.23
3	15,000	13,000	2,000	1.15
4	17,500	18,500	– 1,000	.95
5	20,000	16,000	4,000	1.25

Risk Analysis

The classical definition of the riskiness of an asset is the probability that the future returns expected will fall below expected levels. This is often measured by the standard deviation or the coefficient of variation of expected returns. In the earlier discussion of the various methods of making capital budget decisions, the only treatment of risk was in the informal aspect of making judgments concerning estimates at various economic life and cash flow amounts. Some situations, however, call for a more formal assessment of risk and the effect of uncertainty. We referred to sensitivity analysis in chapter 3. Sensitivity analysis can be used to calculate a project's NPVs under alternative assumptions to see how sensitive NPV is to changing circumstances.

Projects for which the variability in expected returns is very large require an even more formal approach to risk. Risk analysis attempts to identify the likelihood that events will occur. Risk results from lack of experience, misinterpretation of data, bias in forecasting, errors in analysis, and changes in economic conditions. In the process of project feasibility analysis, a number of variables are usually in question.

More than seven out of ten surveyed companies reported that they employ some type of risk assessment in project analysis. Some of the most common risk techniques are:

1. Risk-adjusted discount rate or rate of return
2. Risk-adjusted cash flows
3. Risk-adjusted payback periods

Risk-Adjusted Discount Rate. One of the most frequently used methods is the risk-adjusted discount rate method. The basic objective of the risk-adjusted discount rate method is to increase the applied discount rate when dealing with risky projects. (If the simple rate-of-return method is being used, the cutoff rate is raised to allow for a greater cushion for risky projects.) The increase in the discount rate (cost of capital) is a risk premium to protect the firm from uncertainty of future cash flows of uncertain investments.

As mentioned earlier, the variability of the probability distributions of expected returns can be estimated. In some cases the probability distribution can be estimated objectively with statistical techniques. In many situations, however, the estimates must be determined by subjective probability distributions. Once the probability distribution has been determined, the variability of the distribution can be measured using standard deviation or coefficient of variation. The project with the larger deviation represents the greater risk and is assigned the higher discount rate.

The higher discount rate reduces the present value of the future benefits and makes it more difficult for a risky investment to achieve a positive NPV. Consequently, marginal projects that are also risky will be rejected.

The risk-adjusted discount rate method is easy to apply but has some disadvantages. Usually the adjusted rate applies to all costs and revenues, even those that can be estimated with relative certainty. The lack of discrimination among the cost and revenue estimates is the major criticism of this method.

Risk-Adjusted Cash Flows. As forecasts are being made to develop the point estimate or most likely estimate, the analyst will incorporate into the estimate the risk he perceives. He then defines the degree of uncertainty in terms of probability of occurrence. For example, an optimistic, most likely, and pessimistic estimate is made taking historical data, environmental analysis, and expected trends into consideration. This three-level method of forecasting was exhibited in chapter 2.

To illustrate, consider the following calculation of the expected value of the cash flows from two projects (table 6–4). Table 6–5 shows the calculation of expected value based on the data of table 6–4.

The expected value of the cash flows of project 1 is $640 instead of the $700 point estimate, whereas the expected value of the cash flows of project 2 is $670 rather than $900. The expected value gives the forecaster and the decision maker a better feeling for the risk involved in the decision.

Table 6–4
Expected Values for Cash Flow Calculations without Adjustment for Risk

Project 1 Cash Flow	Project 2 Cash Flow	State of Economy (Probability)	
850	350	.2	Recession
700	900	.5	Normal
400	500	1.3	Boom
		1.0	

Table 6–5
Expected Values for Cash Flow Calculations with Adjustment for Risk

	Cash Flow	Probability of Economic Condition		Expected Value
Project 1	$850	.2	Recession	$170
	700	.5	Normal	350
	400	.3	Boom	120
		1.0		640
Project 2	$350	.2	Recession	$ 70
	900	.5	Normal	450
	500	.3	Boom	150
		1.0		$670

The risk-adjusted cash flow is generally lower than the best-estimate cash flow. The effect of using a risk-adjusted cash flow in the NFV method of capital budgeting is a lower new present value than would have been obtained by using the best-estimate cash flow. The result is that marginal projects with risky potential benefit are more readily discarded.

Simulation Models. Computer simulation can be used to extend probability concepts in decision making. The use of the computer allows decision makers to estimate, for each of a dozen or so variables of major products, ranges of possible outcomes and the probability distributions for these ranges. The focus might be on sales volume, prices, key cost elements, salvage values, interest-rate fluctuations, or cash flows. A series of outcomes of the project is then developed by the computer simulation. The computer output allows statements to be made such as: "There is a 65 percent likelihood that the net present value of the project will be $200,000," or "There is a one in ten chance that the project will lose $210,000." The sophistication of this type of analysis and the limitless number of variables place obvious limitations on its use.

Cost Analysis for Not-for-Profit Entities. The concept of not-for-profit entities is a broad one, including many different types of economic structures: churches, government organizations, universities, hospitals, charitable institutions, clubs fraternal groups, and cooperatives. Income, the traditional measure of success for a profit-making entity, is less of a measure of efficiency for an organization that does not intend to make profits. Thus traditional break-even analysis is a difficult concept to apply to not-for-profit entities (see chapter 3).

Projects of any economic organization should be evaluated for their ability to meet the objectives of the organization within the budget constraints and incomes generated by the activity. With not-for-profit entities this is complicated by the fact that their services cannot always be expressed in dollar terms.

Benefit/Cost Analysis

Cost analysis for not-for-profit organizations is difficult because some costs are difficult to assign. When a nonprofit organization is choosing between alternative programs that fall within the scope of its objectives, benefit/cost analysis can be helpful. Benefit/cost analysis is a formalized attempt to obtain the maximum benefits from a given level of funding. A community wants the best possible police protection, a university wants the best faculty, the Red Cross wants the most effective blood donor recruiting program that the given level of funding can support. Benefit/cost analysis allows a nonprofit organization to evaluate various alternatives.

Each program can be evaluated on the basis of a comparison of benefit/cost ratios. For example, a public library may be considering the addition of a new business section, a film rental library, or an arts library. These alternatives are exhibited in table 6–6.

Alternatives 1 and 2 both have positive net benefits and benefit/cost ratios greater than one. Alternative 2 has the more favorable benefit/cost ratio. If the library has approximately $80,000 available, however, it should embark on both alternatives. Alternative 3 fails both the net-benefit test and the benefit/cost ratio test. Thus, unless there are other overriding considerations, alternative 3 should be rejected.

The basic disadvantage of this type of analysis is the difficulty of estimating both costs and benefits. Costs are perhaps the easiest part of the equation. Costs of construction, equipment, supplies, salaries, and so forth can usually be accurately estimated. Social costs are more difficult to appraise. On the other hand, benefit analysis poses many difficult problems. As we attempt to identify each type of benefit, we run into some social, aesthetic, and nonmonetary benefits. How these are assigned dollar values radically influences the benefit/cost analysis.

Cost-Effectiveness Analysis

When there is difficulty comparing alternatives on a benefit/cost basis, cost-effectiveness analysis may be appropriate. Cost-effectiveness analysis deals with the effect of variations in cost on benefit. The focus of this analysis is to

Table 6–6
Cost/Benefit Ratio Analysis

Alternative	Benefits	Costs	Net Benefit	Benefit/Cost Ratio
1	$32,500	$28,400	$4,100	1.14
2	48,000	40,000	8,000	1.20
3	17,700	22,800	(5,100)	.78

determine effectiveness of operations rather than trying to see how much more benefit there is than cost.

Summary

This chapter has dealt with methods for making capital budgeting decisions. The final consideration in financial analysis is: "How profitable will the project be?" The concepts of return on investment are essential to answering this question. It is hoped that the analysis will lead to a clear yes or a clear no. In some cases, however, "I don't know" will be the response. To say yes implies that the market exists, costs are identifiable and controllable, the process or service works, the financial returns on the investment are satisfactory, and the uncertainty is tolerable.

Chapter 7 will show how to bring these financial considerations into focus with the considerations of a firm's own purpose and resources. This leads to the climax of the process—a decision about whether the firm should pursue an opportunity.

Part IV
Internal Analysis

7
Aligning Market Opportunities with Organizational Resources

T he analysis described so far enters the decision-making realm in this chapter. At this stage the decision maker must decide which, if any, of the market opportunities represent company opportunities—that is, opportunities the company should pursue.

Special attention is given to the factors that must be analyzed in assessing opportunities and the tools needed for this analysis. A special summary worksheet is provided for assimilating the essential facts from the previous analysis as individual opportunities are analyzed.

Problems versus Opportunities

It is important to differentiate between problems and opportunities, although some of the same types of analysis are appropriate for dealing with both. A *problem* is defined as anything that stands in the way of reaching an objective, whereas an *opportunity* is a chance to improve overall performance. To be experiencing a problem, a firm must have already identified objectives it wants to accomplish and have tried to accomplish them. Failure to meet the expectations spelled out in a statement of objectives is, by definition, a problem. Assuming that realistic objectives have been established, the planner must (1) define the exact nature of the problem, (2) identify alternative courses of action (strategies), and (3) select a course of action (strategy) to solve that problem. For the analyst dealing with existing problems, resources have already been committed; decisions revolve around continuation of the commitment, the extent of additional commitments, and the nature of the commitments.

The analyst dealing with opportunities is in a somewhat different position. Either the company has not been involved in the market prior to the analysis or the company is not experiencing a failure to reach objectives but instead is searching for new markets to enter or ways to improve on current performance.

One distinct feature of opportunity analysis is that it involves alignment of market opportunities with purpose and resources, and in many cases goes beyond the realm of a functional decision because it involves a new commitment of resources. It may be, in fact, that the types of analysis described thus far are the basic inputs into a capital budgeting decision, which is beyond the scope of the analyst's job description.

To evaluate opportunities successfully, the analyst must combine the external and financial analysis with internal analysis, which directly influences a firm's willingness and ability to respond to opportunities. Internal factors include purpose or mission and company resources.

Internal Factors

Purpose

The presence of marketing opportunities is a necessary but not a sufficient condition for action. Management must decide whether it wants to take advantage of the existing opportunity and whether it has the resources to exploit the opportunity successfully. That is, it must decide whether the opportunity in the marketplace represents a company opportunity. Opportunities are always available, but not all companies are equally prepared to handle them. The purpose of the organization has a direct bearing on which market opportunities are pursued, as was pointed out in chapter 2. A company's statement of purpose or mission should be used to evaluate market opportunities. There must be alignment between market activities and purpose. The organization wants to pursue only those ventures that will help it fulfill its overall mission; it should reject those that do not.

If, for example, a company's mission is defined as developing high-quality coal, then the identification of a market segment that needs a low-quality coal product in large quantities should not be viewed as a company opportunity regardless of how attractive that segment appears in terms of market potential and lack of competition. Trying to serve the needs of such a segment is in direct opposition to what the company has stated as its mission; such an opportunity must be rejected.

Company Resources

Given that an opportunity is consistent with purpose, the firm's resources must be analyzed to determine the company's ability to respond to an opportunity. At least four types of resources must be analyzed.

(1) **Marketing Resources.** A firm's ability to take advantage of opportunities requires personnel with the marketing skills necessary to develop and execute effective marketing strategies. A good product does not guarantee success.

The old adage "Build a better mousetrap and the world will beat a path to your door" is just not true. Good marketing is the result of good marketers. Many firms that were successful in the industrial market have failed in the consumer market because of a lack of marketing know-how. If a firm does not have adequate marketing skills available within its own organization, its financial resources must be sufficient to acquire the marketing personnel or it must seek the acquisition of a successful firm already positioned in the market that has strong marketing abilities.

An example of the influence of marketing resources on a firm's success is illustrated by a large chemical company's experience with a new consumer product. For years, this company has been a leader in manufacturing and marketing chemical products aimed at the industrial market. Several years ago the firm developed a new cleaning compound and decided to sell it in the consumer market. They were unsuccessful in this attempt because of a lack of experience in marketing consumer products. This product was sold to a consumer goods firm, which marketed the product successfully. Thus it was the original firm's inexperience in marketing consumer goods that caused their failure, not the absence of an opportunity.

(2) **Physical Resources.** Two distinctly different physical resource elements affect a firm's ability to handle new opportunities—productive capability and technological agility. Actual production capacity is influenced by previous commitments to acquire plant and equipment. In the short run this capacity is usually fixed, but it can be altered over time for new strategic opportunities. The technology available during the short run is also considered fixed, and therefore a firm currently either must have both the capacity and the technology or must have the ability to contract with firms that do. A watch manufacturer with capacity may not be able to enter the electronic watch market because of the firm's current pin lever watch technology. Unless the firm subcontracts for component parts, it could not exploit this market opportunity until it acquired new technology. In that situation, financial resources would also be an enabling factor.

The importance of productive resources is evident in what has happened in the watch industry over the past ten years. The watch industry was built around pin lever watch technology. Bulova departed from this technology and developed its Accutron watch with a tuning fork. This was the first of a rash of technological changes, including, of course, the electronic watch. As technology developed, the price of the electronic watch declined and new competitive forces were at work in the industry.

Many firms were unable to enter the competitive electronic watch market because they did not have the necessary productive technology. Other firms were able to break into a new market because of their production technology and capacity in electronic components.

(3) **Financial Resources.** The total amount of financial resources a firm has available and the process through which these funds are allocated influence the firm's ability to enter a market effectively. In some industries there are insurmountable financial barriers for all but the largest companies—automobile manufacturers, for example. Not only are productive resources capital-intensive, but marketing expenditures are also at a high level. Also, although some opportunities appear attractive, the hurdle rate used in the capital budgeting process may be too high. Adequate financial sources must be available to underwrite both production and marketing activities or the firm must have easy access to financial markets before some opportunities can be undertaken.

The absence of financial resources has been the downfall of many companies that had both the production and the marketing resources to be successful. A well-known example is W.T. Grant's department stores. This national chain of department stores was closed in the 1970s because of overextended consumer credit. Grant's simply did not have the financial resources to absorb the bad debt losses and was therefore forced into bankruptcy.

Adequate financial resources enabled Southwest Airlines to operate in the Dallas–Houston–San Antonio markets for the first two years while building up enough patronage to sustain a profitable operation. The low sales revenue and high operating costs during the first two years were anticipated, and the financial revenues permitted continued operation. Thus a firm's current financial position plus its ability to enter capital markets successfully directly influences its ability to pursue opportunities.

(4) **Managerial Resources**

The other important part of the resource base that must be analyzed is managerial resources. This was referred to earlier in terms of matching skills. Management's willingness to take risk, their values, skills, age, and experience are all important aspects of an organization's ability to respond to opportunities.

Financial resources can be used to offset managerial shortcomings if new managers are hired for opportunities that represent a distinct departure from current operations. This was pointed out in chapter 2 with respect to conglomerate diversification.

Table 7–1 illustrates one format for evaluating market opportunities by taking into consideration organizational resources. Each factor—production, marketing, finance, and management—is rated in relation to an opportunity on a scale ranging from very good to very poor. The values assigned to each rating—5 for very good, 4 for good, and so on—permit the rating for each opportunity to be quantified, which enables the analyst to compare several opportunities on a quantitative basis. Production, financial, and marketing personnel should be used to evaluate their respective functions in relation to each opportunity. An alternative approach is to analyze these resources in relation

Table 7–1
Company Resource Evaluation Matrix

	Rating				
Factors Evaluated	*Very Good* (5)	*Good* (4)	*Fair* (3)	*Poor* (2)	*Very Poor* (1)
Production					
Physical facilities					
Labor skills					
Technological capabilities					
Raw material supplies					
Production value					
Marketing					
Marketing skills					
Distribution facilities					
Channel availability					
Marketing score					
Finance					
Fixed capital requirements					
Work capital requirements					
Return on investment					
Finance score					
Managerial					
Number					
Depth					
Experience					
Total Rating					

Source: Adapted from Stewart H. Rewoldt, James R. Scott, and Martin R. Warshaw, *Introduction to Marketing Management* (Homewood, Ill.: Richard D. Irwin, Inc., 1977), pp. 257, 261.

to the opportunity as a strength or weakness. As shown in table 7–2 for each strength and weakness identified, strategic implications are drawn.

Analysis of strengths and weaknesses flows logically from the identification of these resources relative to the opportunity. Each of these resources, when evaluated within this framework, can be labeled as a strength or a weakness, and the implications of that strength or weakness for a specific opportunity must be evaluated.

Ranking Opportunities

Table 7–3 presents a worksheet for summarizing the results of the analysis and ranking the various market opportunities. It is important to develop a comprehensive view of each opportunity by looking at all the various elements that have been analyzed together rather than examining one element—market potential, for example—and then making a decision on the basis of that factor alone.

Table 7–2
Analysis of Strengths and Weaknesses

Factor	Opportunity Implication

A. *Marketing resources*
  1. Strengths:
    Established channels of
    distribution for consumer
    products.
	New product could
	use the same channels.

2. Weaknesses:
    No in-house advertising personnel
    and dependence on agency relationship.
	Product needs strong advertising
	effort—must use ad agency.

B. *Financial resources*
  1. Strengths:
    Good cash position and strong
    price/earnings ratio.
	Consumers need installment
	plans.

2. Weaknesses:
    Higher than average debt/equity
    ratio.
	Must fund through internal
	sources

C. *Physical resources*
  1. Strengths:
    High level of quality control
    technology.
	Go for quality end of
	market.

2. Weaknesses:
    Long down times for product
    changes.
	Must offer limited designs.

D. *Managerial Resources*
  1. Strengths:
    Strong process research
    and development staff.
	Cost-effectiveness in
	production.

2. Weaknesses: No experience with product.	Hire new management team.

It is not one factor by itself that determines the attractiveness of an opportunity but the composite effect of all the factors.

To help quantify the attractiveness of the various opportunities, numbers can be assigned to each for each factor evaluated. For example, if four opportunities are evaluated, the numbers 1 through 4 can be used to rank each opportunity on a given factor. If two opportunities appear to be equal on a given factor, the same number is assigned to each opportunity. If lower numbers are used to indicate higher rankings—that is, if 1 represents the highest rank—the opportunity with the lowest overall score represents the most desirable opportunity for the firm.

As was pointed out earlier, it is not a matter of choosing only one opportunity. A firm with adequate resources may choose several and develop strategies appropriate for each. The result of this type of analysis is recognition of the differences between opportunities and what this implies in terms of the strategies and resources required by a given opportunity.

Table 7–3
Summary of Opportunity Analysis Worksheet

| | | Opportunity Identification | |
| | | Characteristics of Opportunity 1 | Characteristics of Opportunity 2 |
Opportunity			
Factors Analyzed:	*Basic Questions Answered:*	Opportunity Rank	
Environmental	Are the general factors in the environment favorable to this market opportunity?		
Market	What are the specific market factors and are they favorable to this opportunity?		
Market potential	How many consumers are in this opportunity and what are potential sales?		
Competitive analysis	Do we have or can we have differential advantage in this opportunity?		
Revenue/cost analysis	Do we have a good estimate of the revenues and costs involved?		
Profitability analysis	What level of capital expenditures are needed to compete successfully? What is the potential ROI?		
Alignment with purpose/mission	Would going after this opportunity be in line with overall purpose/mission?		
Alignment with resources: Marketing Production Finance Managerial	Do we have or can we acquire the marketing, financial, production, and managerial resources required by this opportunity?		
Other factors Economic Technological Political and legal Cultural and social	Is each of these factors favorable or unfavorable in relation to each opportunity?		
Total score			

Source: Adapted from Robert E. Stevens, *Strategic Marketing Plan Master Guide* Englewood Cliffs, N.J.: Prentice-Hall, 1982), p. 73.

Summary

This chapter concludes the market opportunity analysis. The analyst should have developed a complete data base on environmental factors, market factors, competition, revenue, cost, and return on investment. At this point, decisions must be made concerning which opportunities, if any, will be sought.

The data base that can be developed by performing these types of analyses is the basis for making decisions and is helpful in strategy selection. As new opportunities are identified, the analysis process described previously should become standard procedure and a prerequisite to decision making with respect to these opportunities.

Appendixes

Appendix A
Sources of Data for Market Opportunity Analysis

Industry/Market Data Sources

American Statistics Index: A Comprehensive Guide and Index to the Statistical Publications of the U.S. Government. Published monthly by the Congressional Information Service, this source indexes statistical publications of federal agencies and is a useful starting point for obtaining market data.

Ayer Directory of Publications. Published annually by Ayer Press, this source is a comprehensive listing of newspapers, magazines, and trade publications of the United States (by states), Canada, Bermuda, the republics of Panama and the Philippines, and the Bahamas.

Bureau of the Census Catalog. (U.S. Government Printing Office). Published quarterly, this source is a comprehensive guide to Census Bureau publications on agriculture, foreign trade, governments, population, and the economic census.

Business Conditions Digest, Bureau of Economic Analysis, Department of Commerce (U.S. Government Printing Office). Published monthly, this source gives indications of business activity in table and chart form.

Business Cycle Developments, Bureau of the Census (U.S. Government Printing Office). Published monthly, this source provides some seventy business activity indicators that give keys to general economic conditions.

Business Periodicals Index. This source lists articles by subject heading from 150 or more business periodicals. It also suggests alternative key words that can be used to determine a standard of relevance in environmental analysis.

Business Statistics, Department of Commerce. Published biannually, this source is a supplement to the *Survey of Current Business*. It provides information from some twenty-five hundred statistical series, starting in 1939.

Census of Business (U.S. Government Printing Office). Published every five years, this source supplies statistics on the retail, wholesale, and service trades. The census of service trade compiles information on receipts, legal form of organization, employment, and number of units by geographic area.

Census of Housing (U.S. Government Printing Office). Also published every ten years, this source provides information on types of structures, size, condition, occupancy, monthly rent, average value, and equipment contained by city blocks.

Census of Manufacturers (U.S. Government Printing Office). Published every five years, this source presents manufacturers by type of industry. It contains detailed industry and geographic statistics, such as number of establishments; quantity of output; value added in manufacture; employment; wages; inventories; sales by customer class; and fuel, water, and energy consumption.

Census of Retail Trade (U.S. Government Printing Office). Taken every five years in the years ending in 2 and 7, this source provides information on 100 retail classifications arranged by Standard Industrial Classification (SIC) numbers. Statistics are compiled on number of establishments, total sales, sales by product line, size of firms, employment, and payroll for states, SMAs, counties, and cities of 2,500 or more.

Census of Selected Service Industries (U.S. Government Printing Office). Taken every five years in the years ending in 2 and 7, this source compiles statistics on 150 or more service classifications. Information on the number of establishments, receipts, payrolls, and so forth are provided for various service organizations.

Census of Transportation (U.S. Government Printing Office). Taken every five years in the years ending in 2 and 7, this source presents three specific surveys: Truck Inventory and Use Survey, National Travel Survey, and Commodity Transportation Survey.

Census of Wholesale Trade (U.S. Government Printing Office). Taken every five years in the years ending in 2 and 7, this source provides statistics of 118 wholesale classifications. Information includes numbers of establishments, sales, personnel, payroll, and the like.

Commodity Yearkbook. Published annually by the Commodity Research Bureau, this source supplies data on prices, production, exports, stocks, and so forth for 100 commodities.

County and City Data Book, Bureau of the Census (U.S. Government Printing Office, 1972). This publication gives statistics on population, income, education, employment, housing, and retail and wholesale sales for various cities, SMSAs, and counties.

County Business Patterns, Departments of Commerce and Health, Education and Welfare. Published annually, this source gives statistics on the number of businesses by type and their employment and payroll broken down by county.

Directories of Federal Statistics for Local Areas and for States: Guides to Sources, Bureau of the Census. These two directories list sources of federal statistics for local areas and for states, respectively. Topics include population, health, education, income, and finance.

Economic Almanac. Published every two years by the National Industrial Conference Board, this source gives data on population, prices, communications, transportation, electric and gas consumption, construction, mining, and manufacturing output, in the United States, Canada, and other selected world areas.

Economic Indicators, Council of Economic Advisors, Department of Commerce (U.S. Government Printing Office). Published monthly, this source gives current key indicators of general business conditions, such as GNP and personal consumption expenditures.

Fand S. Index. This detailed index on business-related subjects offers information about companies, industries, and products from numerous business-oriented newspapers, trade journals, financial publications, and special reports.

Federal Reserve Bulletin (Washington, D.C.: Federal Reserve System Board of Governors). Published monthly, this publication offers financial data on interest rates, credit, savings, and banking activity; an index of industrial production; and finance and international trade statistics.

Handbook of Economic Statistics, Economics Statistics Bureau. Published anually, this source presents current and historical statistics of U.S. industry, commerce, agriculture, and labor.

Market Analysis: A Handbook of Current Data Sources, by Nathalie Frank (Metuchen, N.J.: Scarecrow Press, 1969. This book offers sources of secondary information broken down on the basis of indexes, abstracts, directories, and so forth.

Market Guide. Published annually by *Editor and Publisher* magazine, this source lists data for 1,500 U.S. and Canadian cities on population, principal industries, number of households, climate, and retail sales and outlets.

Measuring Markets: A Guide to the Use of Federal and State Statistical Data (U.S. Government Printing Office). This publication lists federal and state publications covering population, income, employment, taxes, and sales. It is a useful starting point for the marketing researcher who is interested in locating secondary data.

Merchandising. Published annually in the March issue of this magazine is the "Statistical and Marketing Report," which presents charts and tables of sales, shipments, product saturation and replacement, trade-ins, and import/export figures for home electronics, major appliances, and housewares. Also appearing annually in the May issue is the "Statistical and Marketing Forecast," which gives manufacturer's sales projections for the coming year and is useful in forecasting certain market factors.

Monthly Labor Review. Published monthly by the U.S. Bureau of Labor Statistics, this source compiles trends and information on employment, wages, weekly working hours, collective agreements, industrial accidents, and so forth.

Predicasts (Cleveland, Ohio: Predicasts, Inc.). This abstract gives forecasts and market data, condensed to one line, from business and financial publications, trade journals, and newspapers. It includes information on products, industries, and the economy, and presents a consensus forecast through 1985 for each data series.

Public Affairs Information Services Bulletin (PAIS), similar but not identical to the *Business Periodicals Index*, this source includes more foreign publications as well as many books, government publications, and many nonperiodical publications.

Rand McNally Commercial Atlas and Marketing Guide (Chicago: Rand McNally Company). Published annually, this source contains marketing data and maps for some 100,000 cities and towns in the United States. It includes such areas as population, auto registrations, basic trading areas, manufacturing, transportation, and related data.

Reader's Guide to Periodical Literature. This index presents articles from magazines of a general nature, such as *U.S. News and World Report, Time,* and *Newsweek.* It also suggests alternative key words that provide initial insight into the nature of the environment.

Sales Management Survey of Buying Power. Published annually by *Sales Management* magazine, this source provides information such as population, income, and retail sales, again broken down by state, county, and SMSA, for the United States and Canada.

Standard and Poor's Industry Survey. Published annually, this source offers current surveys of industries and a monthly "Trends and Projections" section that is useful in forecasting market factors.

Standard and Poor's Trade and Securities Statistics. Published monthly by Standard and Poor's Corporation, this source contains statistics on banking, production, labor, commodity prices, income, trade, securities, and so forth.

Statistical Abstract of the United States, Bureau of the Census (U.S. Government Printing Office). Published annually, this source serves as a good initial reference for other secondary data sources. It includes data tables covering social, economic, industrial, political, and demographic subjects.

Statistics of Income, Internal Revenue Service. Published annually, this source gives balance sheet and income statement statistics, prepared from federal income tax returns of corporations and broken down by major industry, asset size, and so forth.

Survey of Buying Power (New York. Sales Management, Inc.) Published annually, this source gives information on population, income, and retail sales for each county and city of 10,000 population or greater in the United States, Canada, and Mexico.

Survey of Current Business, Bureau of Economic Analysis, Department of Commerce (U.S. Government Printing Office). Published monthly, this source presents indicators of general business, personal consumption expenditures, industry statistics, domestic trade, earnings, and employment by industry, real estate activity, and so forth.

U.S. Industrial Outlook (U.S. Government Printing Office). Published annually, this source provides a detailed analysis of approximately two hundred manufacturing and nonmanufacturing industries. It contains information on recent development, current trends, and a ten-year outlook for the industries. This source is useful in forecasting the specific marketing factors of a market analysis.

Wall Street Journal Index. Published monthly, this source lists general news by subject as it has occurred in this business paper.

Consumer Data Sources

Census of the Population (U.S. Government Printing Office). Taken every ten years, this source reports the population by geographic region, with detailed breakdowns according to demographic characteristics such as sex, marital status, age, education, race, income, and so forth.

Consumer Market and Magazine Report. Published annually by Daniel Starch, this source describes the household population of the United States with respect to a number of demographic variables and consumption statistics. The profiles are based on a large probability sample and provide good consumer behavioral and socioeconomic characteristics.

Crest Report (Chain Restaurant Eating Out Share Trends). Quarterly Supplement to *Food Service Trends*, published by the National Restaurant Association. Survey designed to track expenditures and behavior in commercial segment of the food service industry.

Food Service Trends. Published by the National Restaurant Association. Wholesale Food Price Index and its percentage change are given for farm products, processed foods, and feeds, as shown on page 10 of the June 1979 *Food Service Trends* publication of the National Restaurant Association.

Guide to Consumer Markets. Published annually by the Conference Board, this source provides data on consumer behavior under the following headings: population, employment, income, expenditures, production and distribution, and prices.

Historical Statistics of the U.S. from Colonial Times to 1957. This source, prepared as a supplemental volume to the *Statistical Abstract,* provides data on social, economic, and political aspects of life in the United States. It contains consistent definitions and thus eliminates incompatibilities of data in the *Statistical Abstracts* caused by dynamic changes over time.

Marketing Information Guide. Published monthly by the Department of Commerce, this source lists recently published studies and statistics that serve as a useful source of current information for marketing researchers.

Competitive Data Sources

Almanac of Business and Industrial Financial Ratios. Published annually by Prentice-Hall, this source lists a number of businesses, sales, and certain operating ratios for several industries. The computations are from tax returns, supplied by the IRS, and the data allow comparison of a company's financial ratios with those of competitors of similar size.

Directory of Corporate Affiliations. Published annually by National Register Publishing Company, Inc., this source lists approximately three thousand parent companies and their sixteen thousand divisions, subsidiaries, and affiliates.

Directory of Intercorporate Ownership. Published in 1974 by Simon and Schuster, volume 1 contains parent companies, with divisions, subsidiaries, overseas subsidiaries, and U.S. companies owned by foreign firms. Volume 2 provides an alphabetical listing of all the entries in volume 1.

Fortune Directory. Published annually by *Fortune* magazine, this source presents information on sales, assets, profits, invested capital, and employees for the 500 largest U.S. industrial corporations.

Fortune Double 500 Directory. Published annually in the May–August issues of *Fortune* magazine, this source offers information on assets, sales, and profits of 1,000 of the largest U.S. firms; the 50 largest banks; life insurance companies; and retailing, transportation, utility, and financial companies. In addition, this source ranks foreign firms and banks.

Middle Market Directory. Published annually by Dun & Bradstreet, this source lists companies with assets in the range of $500,000–$999,999. The directory offers information on some thirty thousand companies' officers, products, sales, and number of employees.

Million Dollar Directory. Published annually by Dun & Bradstreet, this source offers the same information as the *Middle Market Directory,* but for companies with assets over $1 million.

Moody's Industrial Manual. Published annually, this source provides information on selected companies' products, history, merger and acquisition record, principal plants and properties, and principal offices, as well as seven years' worth of financial statements and statistical records.

Moody's Manual of Investments. This source documents historical and operational data on selected firms and five years' worth of their balance sheets, income accounts, and dividend records.

Moody's Manuals. This source list includes manuals entitled *Banks and Finance, Municipals and Governments, Public Utilities, and Transportation,* which contain balance sheet and income statements for various companies and government units.

Reference Book of Corporate Managements. Published annually by Dun & Bradstreet, this source lists twenty-four hundred companies and their thirty thousand officers and directors.

Sheldon's Retail Directory of the United States and Canada. Published annually by Phelon, Sheldon & Marsar, Inc., this source supplies the largest chain, department, and specialty stores by state and city (and by Canadian province and city). This source also includes merchandise managers and buyers.

Standard and Poor's Register of Corporations, Directors and Executives. Published annually by Standard & Poor's this source provides officers, sales, products, and number of employees for some thirty thousand U.S. and Canadian corporations.

State Manufacturing Directories. Published for each state, these sources give company addresses, products, officers, and the like by geographic location.

Thomas Register of American Manufacturers. Published annually by the Thomas Publishing Company, this source lists specific manufacturers of individual products as well as each company's address, branch offices, and subsidiaries.

Wall Street Journal Index. Published monthly, this source lists corporate news alphabetically by firm name as it has occurred in the *Wall Street Journal*.

Cost Data Sources

Annual Survey of Manufacturers (U.S. Government Printing Office). Based on a sample of 70,000, it collects industry statistics normally requested by the *Census of Manufacturers*, but includes more detailed information on assets, capital expenditures, retirements, depreciation, supplemental labor costs, and costs of purchased services on an annual basis.

Business Publication Rates and Data. Published by Standard Rate & Data Service, Inc., this index lists various trade publication sources.

Census of Manufacturers (U.S. Government Printing Office, 1977). This census of manufacturers in the United States provides statistics for each state, SCSA, SMSA, county, and selected cities. It includes employment, payrolls, inventories, capital expenditures, assets, retirements, rental payments, depreciation, value added, and so forth.

Economic Census (U.S. Government Printing Office). A comprehensive and periodic canvass of the nation's industrial and business activities, taken by the Census Bureau every five years. In addition to providing the framework for forecasting and planning, these censuses provide weights and benchmarks for indexes of industrial production, productivity, and price. Management uses these in economic or sales forecasting; analyzing sales performance; allocating advertising budgets; locating plants, warehouses, and stores; and so forth.

Encyclopedia of Association (Gale Research Company, 1972). This work may acquaint a researcher with various associations for cost data pertaining to the desired industry.

Moody's Investors Services, Inc. (New York: Standard & Poor's Corporation). This is a financial reporting source about many large firms.

Special Tabulations of data collected in the 1977 Census of Manufacturers are available in summary form on a cost basis. They contain confidential information, including facts about individual business establishments. Inquiries should be directed to the chief of the Industry Division, Bureau of the Census, Washington, D.C. 20233.

Standard Corporation Records. (New York: Standard & Poor's Corporation). This publication includes financial reporting data for the larger firms.

Appendix B
Sample Market Opportunity
Analysis Reports

T his appendix contains three separate sample reports that incorporate the techniques discussed earlier in the book. The first study was completed for a large, diversified company in the petroleum industry. This report not only analyzes the opportunity from a market standpoint but also assesses the company resources that could be used to enter the market. Note that the report was completed in 1981, before the current oil crisis.

The other two sample reports are for new businesses. Thus the internal analysis relating the opportunities to the company's operations was not appropriate. These reports concentrated on carefully identifying market demand, costs, and return on investment opportunities. One of the studies was for a manufacturing operation and the other was for a service operation.

Market Opportunity Analysis:
Urethane Impellers

Prepared for
Blaho, Inc.

Prepared by
Tulsa Market Research Group,
P.O. Box 700895,
Tulsa, OK 74170
(918)-493-3787

Tulsa, Oklahoma
July, 1981

Executive Summary

Is there sufficient demand to justify entry into the market?

Yes. Blaho, Inc., has a guideline that specifies new markets must have potential sales of $500,000 to be acceptable. This analysis derives potentials in three market segments of the total mud pump market. The segments were differentiated on the basis of their needs. They are the replacement market segment, the TRW Mission market segment, and the other manufacturers. Their market potentials were shown to be $931,100, $780,000, and $334,285, respectively. As can be seen, the first two segments easily satisfy the guideline set down by management, so there is sufficient demand to justify entry into the market.

Will the cost of operations be sufficiently low to justify entry?

Yes. Blaho, Inc., has excess production capacity, a factor that originally prompted the search for new markets. The plant operates with high and relatively unalterable fixed costs, near the break-even point. Therefore, the cost of operations would bé the additional variable costs of producing the new product. The overall effect of accepting the new product innovation would be to lower the existing cost of operations and greatly magnify earnings. This is so because fixed costs would be spread over the additional volume of new production.

Will the return on investment be sufficiently high to justify entry?

Yes. The analysis shows that because of excess production capacity in a batch-type process, existing equipment and plant facilities can be used more efficiently. No new investment in plant or equipment is necessary. Therefore, return on investment (though quantifiable) is high. The return would be the additional cash flows brought forth in the analysis, at no additional investment.

How should the market be approached?

The analysis has shown that Blaho, Inc., should first approach TRW Mission and try to establish rapport with Another Company, because they produce 75 percent of the centrifugal pumps used in pumping drilling mud. They should attempt to co-develop the technology necessary with Another Company, which is an industry leader in this technology; has elaborate computerized testing facilities; and will pay for all costs involved with designing, molding, tooling, and testing. Blaho, Inc., should therefore attempt to co-develop the first prototype pump, to be tested, with Another Company.

   Blaho, Inc., should not attempt to go directly to the replacement market segment. This would be to the detriment of sales to the OEM market segments, because the OEMs collectively control 100 percent of the replacement market. Blaho, Inc., should enter into some sort of exclusive dealership or other contractual agreement with the OEMs to reach the replacement market.

Blaho, Inc., should attempt to become established in the mud pump market with a urethane impeller by co-developing the product and the technology with TRW Mission.

Purpose of the Study

It is the purpose of this study to investigate an opportunity afforded to Blaho, Inc. The investigation will follow orderly procedures in obtaining data, analyzing those data, arriving at reasonable conclusions, and reporting those conclusions in a scholarly fashion so that management can make a decision to accept or reject the opportunity.

Statement of the Opportunity

The exact nature of the opportunity afforded to Blaho, Inc., can be defined in one question: Should the company produce and market urethane impellers for centrifugal mud pumps?

Based on estimates of large excess production capacity and idle time over the ensuing long-run planning horizon, the company has determined that it wants to and is able to pursue opportunities for growth in new urethane markets. This strategy is consistent with the purpose of Blaho, Inc., dated January 4, 1984:

1. To fulfill the scope, purpose, and objectives of the corporation as they apply to urethane products.

2. To manufacture high-quality, proprietary urethane parts at the lowest possible costs and to deliver the same dependably.

3. To produce market-engineered urethane products for custom accounts in such a way that the costs of proprietary items will be lowered while the custom customer is satisfied.

4. To increase total plant output, which will yield an additional large income by taking advantage of huge operation leverage.

Since the plant experiences more than proportionate income-to-cost increases with volume increases in production, it is in its best interest to locate the mud pump market. These questions also are directly related to the purpose of this study, and they define the information needs more specifically.

External Analysis

This section focuses on developing an understanding of factors that influence the mud pump market. The analysis seeks to provide initial insight into the nature of the environment that Blaho, Inc., is attempting to enter.

Since the mud pump market is a submarket of the larger market for oil drilling equipment, this anlaysis is oil-fact-based; it encompasses a wide variety of factors pertianing to oil drilling. These factors either directly or indirectly influence, or could potentially influence, the market for hydrocarbon recovery. The factors are useful in developing a general understanding of how Blaho, Inc., and urethane products fit into the oil drilling market.

The anlaysis starts with a historical view and then looks at general environmental factors affecting the drilling industry. This background is provided to give a clearer understanding of the mud pump market.

Historical Perspective. The analysis begins with a historical perspective on the industry. In early civilizations the sole source of energy was wood. Overutilization in the sixteenth century caused shortages and consequent changes in sources. The use of coal as an energy source began at this time. Coal became a prominent energy source in the nineteenth century with the advent of labor-saving devices, primarily with steam power. In the later half of the nineteenth century, the need for development of electric generation capabilities increased. Particular impetus came from the invention of the internal combustion engine. Crude oil was desperately needed, and the age of petroleum began.

Petroleum use has increased tremendously in the late twentieth century. Up to 1948 the United States exported crude oil; domestic production exceeded consumption. By 1954, when the United States was importing 15 percent crude, it was announced as government policy that to import more than 15 percent would be to affect the U.S. national defense and world posture. Nevertheless, petroleum use gradually increased by 1973. Imports rose to 25 percent of use. Today the United States imports 18.7 million barrels of crude per day, or 50 percent of its consumption. The United States spends $10 million per hour per day for crude, or $90 billion per year.

The increase in energy use, compounded yearly, was 4 percent until 1980, when there was a glut in crude supplies. Any drastic changes in crude usage in the short run would cause chaos to the developed economies of the world, particularly to the United States. The initial stages of chaos could be seen during the gasoline shortage and long gas lines of the 1970s.

Environmental Factors. Percentage increase in energy use parallels percentage growth in GNP. Petroleum has experienced a 700 percent price increase in seven years. This incentive, combined with a ready market for any oil found, has triggered a new wave of capital spending to develop supplies of oil and gas. According to a forecast at Exxon, however, this strong market picture for petroleum activity anticipates only modest growth in energy demand in the United States—1.1 percent per year during the 1980s and 1.6 percent during the 1990s. But while energy demand rises 30 percent, from 37.4 million barrels per day in 1980 to 50.3 million in 2000, U.S. demand for oil will decline slightly. Dependence on oil imports will rise during the 1980s as synthetic fuels come on stream to supplement shrinking domestic supplies. Imports of gas will double during the next two decades but will also be supplemented strongly by synthetics. Alternative and synthetic fuels will be considered later in this chapter.

Drilling. How does this affect the drilling industry and, consequently, the mud pump market? It is highly unlikely that the drilling industry will be adversely affected in the immediate future. The drilling industry has its best year ever, 1980—a twenty-five-year record. Common indicators like wells, footage, and rig count show higher activity than ever before. And industry is primed for an even busier year in 1981. The drilling boom dating from the mid-1970s continues its upward spiral, with no letup in sight. The surge in drilling, in its seventh year, is beginning to bear fruit. Under phased decontrol, higher real prices for oil and gas provide a sharp stimulus to exploration.

This surge is not just a domestic increase. Drilling activity continues on the upswing around the globe. Areas covered by Hughes Tool Company's quarterly international count showed a tally of 4,062 active rotary rigs at the end of 1979—a 13.5 percent advance from a year earlier and a 3.6 percent increase from the previous quarter. The count covered noncommunist regions as well as action off China.

This surge is expected to cause a sharp rise in demand for U.S. oil equipment. The value of market demand for U.S. manufactured oilfield machinery and equipment is seen as doubling during the period 1978–1988.

Enhanced recovery operations and offshore drilling/production will pace the increase, says Frost & Sullivan Inc. (FSI) in its market report. FSI predicts that market demand for U.S. oil field machinery and equipment will grow 7.5 percent per year through 1982 and 6.5 percent a year therafter through 1988. While demand rises sharply, however, U.S. manufacturers will face more overseas competition that will trim the market share for U.S. firms.

What will an increase in equipment demand do to the supply? The answer is uncertain. Reports are contraditory. Most sources feel that the surge in U.S. drilling is squeezing supplies of oil field equipment. Others feel that ample drilling equipment is foreseen for the busy years ahead.

Many industry executives believe that supplies of domestically produced equipment will grow tighter as the pace of drilling activity picks up speed. This tight market might force operators to import equipment. In addition, executives believe that the push to develop a synthetic-fuels industry will put added pressure on supplies of a variety of processing equipment. And the surge in U.S. defense spending spells more competition for manufacturing manpower and materials. It all adds up to what one executive calls "a big question": Can U.S. oil field equipment suppliers expand quickly enough to keep pace with growing markets for their goods?

Another source feels that suppliers can meet the large increase and that rises in drilling activity in response to oil and gas decontrol will not strain equipment supplies and create shortages like those of 1973–1974. How? For one thing, suppliers have already increased their productive capacity significantly since the last series of shortages. In addition, the business climate has changed. In 1973 and 1974 the housing and automobile industries competed with the petroleum business for cement and steel. These industries are now in a slump, so suppliers, with their capacities enlarged to meet demand, now have access to the basic raw materials they need. Finally, operators are plannng more effectively than they did in the early 1970s. All these factors should combine to help operators and contractors maintain the anticipated growth in drilling activity.

The latest Commerce Department survey lists the growth potential for the U.S. petroleum supply industry as excellent during the next five years. Total shipments by the oil field machinery industry alone were $6.0 billion last year, a 16 percent increase from 1979. By 1984 shipments are expected to reach $6.49 billion, a compound growth rate of 4.5 percent a year in constant 1979 dollars.

An interesting, newly rediscovered use is in shallow-drilling equipment, specifically in percussion drills. The percussion rig differs from conventional mud rotaries mainly in depth of footage drilled. These rigs go down to depths of only about two thousand feet. This type of drill has a lower initial rig and equipment cost, faster drilling rates, and cheaper drilling cost per foot than conventional mud rotaries that go down to depths of five thousand to six thousand feet and more. The percussion rigs are designed to reach shallow oil and gas reservoirs at a cost of about $4 per foot. Conventional rigs cost $7 to $10 per foot.

The percussion rigs bring cuttings to the surface by using compressed air instead of drilling mud. Therefore, they usually have no mud pumps. The percussion rigs drill shallow holes as fast as 200 feet per hour with air circulation. For these reasons the rigs are used on a wildcat basis to poke into potentially productive zones.

The rigs are gaining popularity each day. At the end of January 1981 there were an estimated 40 in operation in Oklahoma alone. The Hughes Tool Company weekly count of active rotary rigs does not include percussion rigs. This count was 536 active rigs in Oklahoma at the end of January 1981. Percussion rigs then represent approximately 7 percent of the active rigs in Oklahoma.

A spokesman for one company who makes percussion rigs, said, "They're going in there just about as fast as we can build them." The impact of these rigs on the mud pump market is undeterminable at this time, but others believe that higher prices have made smaller reservoirs at shallower depths just as attractive as larger reservoirs at deeper depths.

In summary, virtually all areas of drilling activity and drilling technology are enjoying a magnificent period. More money is being spent on exploration, drilling, and research, and more progress is being made. Service companies that supply the industry have greatly expanded their capacity. The output of services, consumables, and drilling equipment is the highest ever, as is demand. Scattered backlogs exist. For example, TRW Mission currently has a backlog of four thousand mud pumps. They sell approximately a thousand per month, and they anticipate a 30–40 percent increase in this number this next year. The outlook for drilling and associated equipment is bright at least through the early 1980s.

Market Analysis

In the last section the analysis started with a general overview of the drilling industry, followed by a more specific view of the mud pump market. The information presented came from secondary data sources, primarily industry and trade journals and publications.

In this section the analysis becomes even more specific. This section identifies the industrial consumer's (mud pump manufacturer's) needs, based on certain characteristics of the mud pump market. The information presented here is taken from personal interviews conducted during December 1985 with centrifugal pump manufacturers in Houston, Texas, and Oklahoma City, Oklahoma.

The information gathered from these companies was oriented specifically toward the market segments pertaining to mud pumps. These manufacturers make many different types of centrifugal pumps, most of which have applicability in other markets. The needs of industrial consumers in one market are different from the needs of industrial consumers in another market. Since different marketing strategies should be used for each market, and since the information was collected with a focus on centrifugal pumps used to pump drilling mud, the results of this analysis should not be generalized to pumps used outside the oil drilling industry. These results are meant to reflect centrifugal pump manufacurers' needs as they pertain to mud pumps, and to provide insight into the types of strategies needed to meet only these specific needs.

The consumer analysis will consist of a list of three identifying characteristics of the mud pump market segment compiled from the interviews. This information is helpful in developing a qualitative profile of mud pump manufacturers. Information on the demand or quantitative side of the market will then be provided in estimates of the market potential, also derived from the interviews.

The next section includes a competitive analysis for the mud pump market. Since urethane impellers for mud pumps are a relatively new innovation, this analysis is primarily limited to potential competition rather than existing, identifiable competitors. The analysis should be used to try to anticipate the moves of competition when deciding whether or not to pursue the mud pump market, or when deciding what strategy to use. Again, information is taken from interviews of the three potential industrial consumers.

Characteristics and Needs of Potential Customers. The analysis begins by looking at market characteristics of the potential consumers. This approach ensures a consumer-oriented view of the market rather than a product-oriented view. An assessment will then be made of the impact of each consumer characteristics on need satisfaction.

Most industrial consumer characteristics do not differentiate the potential consumers in terms of need satisfaction. The consumers have similar needs that can be satisfied by the same marketing mix or package of strategies. To maximize opportunity for Blaho, Inc., however, it is important to differentiate among these needs. The most notable characteristics that would identify different segments within the mud pump market are the type of organization, the nature of its business, and the size of the organization as measured by the volume of pumps sold per month.

The type of organization and the nature of its business are interrelated. The former characteristic refers to whether or not the company is an original equipment manufacturer (OEM); the latter refers to the replacement market for impellers. Both of these are viable market segments of the total mud pump market, but the replacement market is dominated by original equipment manufacturers. It is unlikely that Blaho, Inc., could enter the replacement market for impellers without going through the OEMs. This might be to the detriment of impeller sales to the OEM segment, for several reasons.

First, manufacturers, collectively, control 100 percent of the replacement market for impellers, and they do not want to jeopardize their sales in this market. This gives rise to the second obstacle for Blaho in entering the replacement market. The manufacturers are somewhat skeptical of Blaho's motives; they fear that Blaho, Inc., might use the technology the OEMs have developed in mud pumps, combine it with urethane, and attempt to sell directly to the replacement market. An incident similar to this occurred a few years ago, with the other Company.

A pump manufacturing company in a western state made a urethane impeller to fit a standard pump. TRW Mission believes much of the pump was copied from the technology they developed for this standard type. Apparently the other company then put the urethane impeller on its own pump in the field. The pump failed, and the company had to send one of its technical representatives halfway across the United States to try to ameliorate the resulting conflict. The pump manufacturer was surprised to see that the failure was caused by a urethane impeller that the manufacturer didn't know existed. Consequently, this company has its doubts about urethane and about the motives of Blaho, Inc.

This leads to a third reason that Blaho, Inc., might have difficulty in directly entering a replacement market. Blaho, Inc., would probably have to work in conjunction with the OEMs to develop the technology necessary for a successful urethane impeller pump. For reasons of potential lost revenues and possible urethane failures, the OEMs are reluctant to share their technology. All these factors differentiate the specific needs of the OEM market segment from those of the replacement market segment of the mud pump market.

The OEMs need to be reassured about urethane's technical workability. They need to be dealt with courteously and with integrity. They need to be made aware of urethane's convenience and the efficiency of urethane and of the value offered by its unique product qualities. Emphasis must be placed on urethane's durability and abrasive resistance, its superiority over steel in the operating conditions of mud pumps. Urethane's dependability can be emphasized by pointing out that it can be made rigid enough to withstand buckling under suction pressures encountered in pumps. The manufacturers typically think of urethane as soft or pliable, like rubber. It can also be pointed out that urethane can increase productivity in the field. This would be a good selling tool for the OEMs to use with their customers. Finally, since urethane costs less than steel, the OEMs can realize economies of purchase and use that will increase their earnings.

To reach the replacement market for urethane impellers, Blaho, Inc., would have to satisfy the aforementioned needs plus other, more specific ones. The OEMs would probably have to be reassured that they would not lose their replacement market sales. This need could be met through an exclusive dealership or some other sort of contractual agreement. Blaho, Inc., will probably have to reach the replacement market through the OEMs by selling urethane replacement impellers to the OEMS, who in turn would sell them to the ultimate users in the field.

The third market segment can be differentiated by size, as measured by pump sales per month. A recent study estimated that one company manufactured and sold 75 percent of the centrifugal pumps used in pumping drilling mud. Other estimates are more conservative; they estimate that that company has 68 to 70 percent of the mud pump market. In addition, 30 percent of the leading company's mud pump sales are international; their pumps can be seen on Chinese and Soviet oil rigs. The leading company sells approximately a thousand mud pumps per month, and they anticipate a 30 to 40 percent increase in this figure over the next year. This level of sales qualifies this company to be classified as a specific market segment within the mud pump market.

The analysis up to now has explored three different potential market segments of the total mud pump market, identified by the type of organization, the nature of its business, and the size of the organization. Specific needs of the segments were then identified. Insight can now be achieved into the different strategies needed to satisfy the specific needs of the different segments. The segments identified were original manufacturers of mud pumps, the replacement market for impellers, and the leading company. The analysis now turns to estimating the annual potential in each market segment.

Market Potential. Market Potential of the major-manufacturer segment can be determined simply by taking their current sales rate and extending it over future horizons. As was mentioned, the leader sells approximately one thousand mud pumps per month. This firm expects a 30 percent increase in this figure over the next year alone, which would mean an estimated sales potential of 15,600 pumps for 1981 (1,000 + 30% *12). Assuming an average steel impeller weighs about 25 pounds, and assuming the ratio of five to one steel to urethane in impeller weight, we can calculate the amount of urethane sales potential to the leader market segment. With these assumptions, we see that the average impeller sold will contain about 5 pounds of urethane (zs/s). Obviously this figure will vary according to the size of the pump sold and the number of different sizes sold. Five pounds is only an average estimate and is subject to change. If the leader sold 15,600 pumps, each containing 5 pounds of urethane, Blaho, Inc.'s potential sales for urethane would be 78,000 pounds to the leader alone (15,600 × 5). Multiplying this figure by an estimated $10/pound selling price for urethane, we see that total dollar potential of urethane for the leader is $780,000 or more, annual (78,000 *$10).

Assuming this figure is 70 percent of the total mud pump market potential, we can easily calculate the potential for the market segment of all other OEMs. If $780,000 is 70 percent of the total market for urethane impellers, then the total market of all OEMs, less that of the leader, is $334,285.

$$0.70x = \$\ 788,000$$
$$x = \$1,114,285$$
$$\$1,114,285 - \$780,000 = \$\ 334,285$$

Estimates for potential of the replacement market segment are a little less tangible. This estimation entails a projection of useful life for inpellers and an evaluation of the current number of impellers (pumps) that are in the field. Useful life of impellers varies with their quality and duration of use on drilling rigs. The average service life for impellers used to pump drilling mud could be as high as three years under general use or as low as two months under intense use. An average useful life is estimated to be about one year under normal operating conditions. Pumps usually do not last more than a year or a year and a half because they are sometimes run twenty-four hours a day. Normal operating conditions vary, but they usually reflect the design of the drilling rig system.

Not all rigs are well designed. Some systems run numerous desanders and desilters off only one or two pumps. This intense use of the pump category shortens its useful service life. The rig system's arrangement varies according to the needs of the driller. If the system has hydrocyclones, each desander and desilter should have its own pump; otherwise it is not well designed. Most rig systems are well designed primarily because production down time is very costly. A well-designed rig system will have four or five pumps; the management of Demco estimates this slightly higher, at five to seven pumps per rig. These figures refer to land rigs; the management of Democ also estimates offshore rigs to have twelve to fourteen pumps. For purposes of this analysis, an average figure of five pumps per onshore rig and thirteen pumps per offshore rig will be used.

By multiplying these figures by the active number of onshore and offshore rigs, the total number of pumps and impellers can be estimated for the U.S. market. Estimating a useful life of one year for impellers, the annual potential for the replacement market segment can be derived.

Each week, the *Oil and Gas Journal* publishes the Hughes rig count. On December 29, 1980, there were 3,077 land rigs in operation in the total United States. Offshore of California there were 21 rigs, offshore of Louisiana 146, and offshore of Texas 82 rigs. This gives a total of 249 rigs operating offhsore in the United States. Using the estimate of average pumps per rig, the total number of pumps offshore can be computed as 15,385 [3,077 *5]. The total number offshore can be computed as 3,237 [249 '13]. The total U.S. mud pump market then is estimated at 18,622 at the year end of 1980. Assuming the useful life of an impeller to be one year, the total potential for the mud pump impeller replacement market is also 18,622.

If all these impellers were made of urethane, total urethane sales in pounds would be 93,110 pounds (18,622 *5—recall that an average impeller was estimated to contain 5 pounds of urethane). Again, using a sales price of $10/pound for urethane, total dollar sales of the replacement market segment can be estimated at $931,100 annually [93,110 *10].

The $931,100 figure of the replacement market segment and the $780,000 figure of the leader market segment, and the $334,285 of the market segment of all OEMs less the leader, together, exceed the guideline of $500,000 potential market sales that is laid down by Blaho, Inc. Total market potential then is

$$\$931,000 + \$780,000 + \$334,285 = \$2,045,395$$

This is the mud pump market's capacity to consume urethane impellers in this one year (see table B–1).

This concludes the development of the consumer profiles. The results of this analysis can be used in subsequent time periods by updating or expanding the estimates. The analysis now turns to a competitive analysis.

Competitive Analysis

From the information gathered in the interviews, it can be said that currently there is no successful competition in the market for urethane impellers. None of the companies interviewed is using urethane for impellers. Competitors have

Table B–1
Overall Market Characteristics

Market Segment	Characteristics	To be Satisfied	Potential
OEMs less the leader	Type of organization	Reassurance of urethane quality, workability, cost-efficiency, and value	$334,285
Replacement	Nature of business	Exclusive dealership or other contractual agreement	$931,100
TRW Mission	Size of organization	General reassurances of all OEMs, pumps, control of all prototypes, potential foundry losses	$780,000

no clearly identifiable strategies for meeting the specific needs of any of the market segments. The one company that attempted to break into the urethane market failed because of its unethical strategy. Although no identifiable competition now exists, however, consideration must be given to potential competitors that could easily enter the market if Blaho, Inc., enters.

Foremost consideration should be given to trying to anticipate the moves of Jones and Sons, a company that has already attempted to make a urethane impeller. Jones and Sons tried to enter the replacement market without meeting the specific need of co-developing technology with the OEMs, and consequently failed. Consideration should also be given to the SWEAT Company. SWEAT has its urethane facilities and is currently making urethane hydrocyclone liners. Consideration should also be given to a company called Beltway, in Wisconsin. Not much is known about Beltway, but it apparently manufactures products with properties similar to urethane. Beltway could possibly have its own urethane facilities.

In addition to these potential competitors, Blaho, Inc., would also want to consider the OEMs. If urethane was successful in mud pump use, it could be reasonably assumed that other competition would enter the market. A likely source of this competition would be the OEMs. Little is known about the OEMs other than those interviewed; these other OEMs might have urethane facilities or be able to acquire them. This would hinge on the success of urethane impellers and on the efficiencies of cost to the OEMs in a make-or-buy decision.

In sum, it can be said that Blaho, Inc., will face potential competition at the manufacturing level. It is at this level that Blaho, Inc., must analyze the market. Competition can be classified as *oligopolistic*—a few suppliers going ·after the same markets. Entry to these markets is difficult for anyone lacking the drilling product technology and the capital to invest in urethane equipment.

This will cause an interdependency among the existing urethane firms. If Blaho, Inc., is successful in penetrating the mud pump segments, it can certainly be assumed that others will follow. Blaho, Inc., should be aware of this and should anticipate the moves of competitors. Blaho, Inc., has the potential for successful entry and exploitation of the marketing opportunity afforded by the mud pump market because of its differential advantage. The firm has an edge over competitors with a process innovation that differentiates Blaho, Inc., and could probably be used for smaller, more standardized impellers, thus giving Blaho, Inc., a greater and higher-quality output at a reduced cost. This, combined with the fact that no one is currently successfully meeting the specific needs outlined in the consumer analysis, give Blaho, Inc., the edge over competition and potential for success.

This concludes the industrial consumer and competitive analysis. The next section will review an opportunity analysis. It will focus on total production, marketing, and financial opportunities of Blaho, Inc., in the mud pump market.

Financial Analysis

The last section showed that Blaho, Inc., has the potential for successful entry into and exploitation of urethane impeller markets for mud pumps. The potential sales of three individual market segments were projected both in dollars and in units. Several characteristics that differentiate the three market segments were identified, as were specific needs to be satisfied in each segment. Blaho, Inc., will have to develop marketing strategies to meet these needs. Decisions will have to be made about which market segments will be sought with what marketing mixes (array of strategies).

This section will estimate the financial impact of these decisions, which is directly in line with the marketing concept of satisfying consumers' needs at a profit. Evaluation of the financial impact of choosing a specific market segment, and the resulting strategy or strategies, will estimate sales, cost of sales, and administrative expenses associated with a market segment before any strategies are implemented. This prevents overly optimistic or pessimistic biases from muddying the strategic planning process.

The approach used in this financial impact evaluation will embrace the concept of using pro forma income statements. Estimates of cash flows to be produced by urethane impeller sales will be computed.

Pro forma analysis begins with the sales forecast. Market segment potentials, in dollars, for urethane impellers were derived in the last section. Total market potentials in each market segment were found to be $780,000 for the leader, $931,100 for the replacement market, and $334,285 for all other OEMs. These figures are the maximum sales for urethane impellers that can be obtained initially in each market segment. It is important to look at the market potentials individually rather than collectively, since the segments are mutually exclusive. for example, initially aiming at the replacement market with one's strategies would probably be to the detriment of potentials in the OEM market segments, since the OEMs collectively control 100 percent of the replacement market.

It is highly unlikely that Blaho, Inc., or any company, will take 100 percent of these markets initially. Therefore, a common procedure to use in estimating sales is the acceptance rate method—estimating the rate at which the various industrial consumers will accept urethane impellers for cast iron impellers. It is reasonable to assume that the acceptance rates will change as revenues and costs change over the course of the urethane impeller's product life cycle. The format is the important point in the sales estimation. Different numbers can be plugged in as acceptance rates to update or modify the sales forecasts over time.

For purposes of this study, an acceptance rate of 50 percent is assumed to be most likely in all segments. An acceptance rate of 25 percent is assumed to be pessimistic, and 75 percent is assumed to be initially optimistic. This is based on the initial order requirements of Blaho, Inc., and on the potentials of the various market segments. Blaho, Inc., has guidelines on new ventures that stipulate that the first commercial order must be at least 2,000 pounds or $20,000, and the following order 10,000 pounds or $80,000. This is also under the condition of a joint research and development agreement that stipulates that Blaho, Inc., would provide the manpower and the industrial consumer would pay the expenses. The key, again, is the format; management can plug in any estimate of acceptance they feel is appropriate.

With the assumed acceptance rate, and the market potentials derived previously, alternative sales forecasts for each market segment can be computed as follows:

TRW Mission Segment—Maximum Potential $780,000

Low forecast	$195,000 (25% of $780,000)
Most likely	$390,000 (50% of $780,000)
High Forecast	$585,000 (75% of $780,000)

Replacement Market—Maximum Potential $931,100

Low forecast	$232,775 (25% of $931,100)
Most likely	$465,550 (50% of $931,100)
High Forecast	$698,325 (75% of $931,100)

All other OEMs—Maximum Potential $334,285

Low Forecast	$ 83,571 (25% of $334,285)
Most likely	$167,143 (50% of $334,285)
High forecast	$250,714 (75% of $334,285)

Sale ranges of approximately $190,000–$590,000, $230,000–$7 million, and $80,000–$250,000 can be estimated for the market segments of the leader, replacement, and all other OEMs, respectively. To derive sales figures for the pro forma income statements, the following probabilities are assigned to each forecast:

Low forecast	0.25
Most likely	0.50
High forecast	0.25
Total	1.00

The expected initial sales revenue (SR) of each market segment can then be computed as follows:

Leader:

E_{SR} = ($195,000) (0.25) + ($390,000) (0.50) + ($585,000) (0.25)

E_{SR} = $48,750 + $195,000 + $146,250

E_{SR} = $390,000

Replacement market:

E_{SR} = ($232,775) (0.25) + ($465,550) (0.50) + ($698,325) (0.25)

E_{SR} = $59,194 + $232,775 + $174,581

E_{SR} = $465,550

All other OEMs:

E_{SR} = ($83,571) (0.25) + ($167,143) (0.50) + ($250,714) (0.25)

E_{SR} = $20,893 + $83,571 + $62,679

E_{SR} = $166,143

These final values ($390,000, $465,550, and $166,143) can be used as the estimated sales revenues to be generated initially from urethane impeller sales in the pro forma income statement.

A pro forma income statement for the three newly proposed market segments is shown in table B–2. The percentage figures are managerial estimates given by Jack Sims, director of marketing at Blaho, Inc. The tax rate assumed is 48 percent. These figures may or may not be accurate; it is the format that is the key. Different figures can be used as situations change. For example, by the time full-scale commercialization has been reached, much new data are available on production costs, marketing costs, and administrative costs. These new data permit a more precise estimate of the profit impact of a chosen strategy.

Table B–2
Pro Forma Income Statements

	Leader Segment	*Replacement Segment*	*All other OEMs Segment*
Sales:	$390,000	$465,550	$166,143
Cost of sales (50%)	195,000	232,775	83,072
Gross margin	$195,000	$232,775	$ 83,071
Expenses:			
Direct selling and marketing (11%)	$ 42,900	$ 51,210	$ 18,276
Depreciation (5%)	19,500	23,278	8,307
Administrative and other manufacturing expenses (7%)	27,300	32,588	11,630
Financial charges (3%)	11,700	13,967	4,984
Total expenses	$101,400	$121,043	$ 43,197
Profit before taxes	$ 93,600	$111,732	$ 39,874
Net profit after taxes	$ 48,672	$ 58,101	$ 20.734
Plus depreciation	+ $ 19,500	+ $ 23,278	+ $ 18,276
Cash flow	$ 68,172		
		$ 81,379	$ 39,010

The format, however, is consistent; it is the key. This format is also in line with a more realistic approach to demand forecsting, which produces a range of sales volumes for new projects.

The estimates used in the pro forma income statement are 50 percent for cost of sales, 11 percent for direct selling and marketing, 5 percent for depreciation, 7 percent for other manufacturing expenses and administrative costs, and 3 percent for financial charges. Some of these expenses should vary spontaneously with sales; others might remain fixed over a relevant range of production or over a specific time period. In any event, the anlaysis shows the initial cash flows to be $69,172, $81,379, and $39,010 from the market segments of the leader, replacement, and all other OEMs, respectively.

Normally, the third step in analyzing the financial impact of a strategy is to compute ROI given the level of cash flow generated by a new product or new strategy. ROI is a commonly used figure for determining the acceptance of a proposed plan. In this specific analysis, no additional capital investment in plant and equipment is needed initially. Blaho, Inc.'s excess production capacity is what made the idea of urethane impellers for mud pumps an attractive venture. Capital is added at a total plant level as sales volume increases permanently, since all the equipment is used to batch process products that have essentially similar characteristics.

Bill Jones, the plant manager, estimates the urethane impeller project to have little initial effect on the urethane plant's total production capacity. Blaho, Inc., uses a stepwise method of increasing the capital investment level. As sales volume rises to new highs, Blaho, Inc., adds additional equipment or expands plant facilities to meet the rising needs. Investment then comes at the different steps or levels depicted in this figure. This level is not expected to increase for some time, and the results of the impeller project will not affect it. The only real investment would be the raw materials used and the increased labor and machine usage. The return would be the cash flows already computed.

This concludes the opportunity analysis of the proposed urethane impeller project. The marketing department must be accountable for producing a plan at an acceptable level of profits, as must all the other departments involved in the strategic planning process. This opportunity analysis has done essentially that.

Using the estimates of size of the market segments derived in the last section, the initial sales of the new product were estimated on the basis of original equipment projections and replacement potentials for iron impellers. An acceptance rate was estimated for the proportion of existing consumers that would switch to the new product when it was introduced on the market. Cash flows were projected—essentially, the net profits after taxes plus depreciation of the three market segments. Return on investment was found to be nonapplicable in this case since no additional investment in plant or equipment would be required.

The next section will summarize the analysis, draw conclusions, and provide implications and recommendations for mangement.

Internal Analysis

Summary of Purpose. This analysis has attempted to evaluate whether Blaho, Inc., should make a urethane part for centrifugal pumps used to pump oil drilling mud. The investigation centered on the needs of the mud pump manufacturers and assessed Blaho, Inc.'s ability to meet those needs, based on the firm's financial, productive, marketing, and management resources.

Review of the Findings. Through personal interviews with several primary mud pump manufacturers, their needs were determined. Generally the OEMs are somewhat skeptical and need to be made aware of the convenience and efficiency of urethane, as well as the value offered by urethane's unique product qualities. The manufacturers need to be assured of urethane's superiority over steel in the operating conditions of mud pumps. Urethane is not only more durable and abrasive-resistant than steel under these conditions; it is also less costly than steel. Instilling an awareness of all these factors defines the needs of the OEMS.

The findings also reveal that the OEMs are not the only market for mud pump parts. There is also a strong replacement market, which also has specific needs. Since the replacement market is currently dominated and controlled by the OEMs, there is a need to approach this market gingerly to avoid losing potential customers in the OEM market segment.

The findings indicate that Blaho, Inc., has the financial, productive, and marketing capabilities to meet the needs defined. This was shown to be true primarily through the excess production capacity of the urethane plant. Financial incentive to meet the need was also demonstrated by the addition to cash flows that the new urethane part would provide, all without additional plant or capital expenditures.

Conclusions and Implications. The ability of Blaho, Inc., to meet the needs of the industrial consumer at a profit indicates that it should pursue the urethane mud pump impeller project. The project's feasibility has been established from a combined viewpoint of Blaho's marketing, production, and financial resources. Determining feasibility, however, is only the first step in marketing a new product. Although everything looks good up to this point, this study has only scratched the surface. There are more "go–no go" stages to consider before the first unit is produced. Marketing a new product requires continuously updated research.

Recommendations for Future Research. Blaho, Inc., will now need to explore what approach to take to establish rapport with the OEMs, in order to produce the first prototype for a field test. This will involve Blaho, Inc., and the OEMs sharing joint costs and technologies. This study has suggested that the attempt be made to establish rapport with the industry leader and to satisfy its needs. The reason was shown to be the leader's size and their lab and technological capabilities.

From this stage on Blaho, Inc., will have to research more thoroughly its internal costs and operations. If and when the technology is developed, Blaho, Inc., will have to define its costs for designs, molds, tooling, and processing. For these reasons again, the leader was suggested as a company to approach because it would pay for all these costs, as stated in its company policy.

Recommendations to Management. It was also recommended that no attempt be made initially to sell directly to the replacement market. To do so would be to risk losing the potential of selling to the OEM segment and the leader, which now control the replacement market.

Discussion of Recommendation. One way to avoid any conflict with the OEMs over the replacement market is first to become established both with a product and with a technology. Since even urethane will wear out in mud pump usage, replacement parts will be needed in the field. As these needs occur, and urethane impellers become more established, Blaho, Inc., will see this as a growing market.

At that point it might be acceptable to sell directly to the end users, but initially this would not work. The OEMs would never share the technology necessary to develop a workable urethane part for their pumps without having an exclusive dealership or other contractual agreement guaranteeing them access to replacement parts. As the market for urethane parts expands with increased drilling, or as the contractual agreements expire, Blaho, Inc., may be able to enter the replacement field. Initially, however, this is not seen as a viable strategy.

Market Opportunity Analysis:
Rollco Packing Company

Prepared by
Tulsa Marketing Research Group,
P.O. Box 700895,
Tulsa, OK 74170
(918) 493-3787

Tulsa, Oklahoma
April, 1986

Executive Summary

There are four major considerations in assessing the economic feasibility of the proposed Rollco Packing Company.

1. Is there sufficient demand for beef and pork products in the three-state market area to justify the establishment of an additional slaughtering operation?

An analysis of population and consumption patterns for the three-state area compared to total output of present slaughtering operations in this three-state area shows a net excess of consumption when stated in animal equivalents of 1,846,750 cattle and 2,373,750 hogs. Projections of future demand indicate a further increase in the consumption of both beef and pork products for the market area. Therefore, it is concluded that there would be ample demand for the output of the proposed facility operating at the level of production of 93,750 hogs and 93,750 cattle annually.

2. Is there sufficient supply of animals in the area of the proposed facility to support the proposed level of output of 93,750 cattle and 93,750 hogs annually?

Although there is a large inventory of cattle and hogs in the three-state area, the number of cattle available for slaughter is considerably lower than the inventory would indicate. The absence of feedlot operations in the area would necessitate the importation of approximately 20 percent of the cattle output of the facility, or approximately 15,000 cattle of the higher grades. With the present marketings of animals within the area and the proposed sales facility at Columbus, U.S.A., it is probably that the 75,000 cattle of lower grades could be acquired within the immediate area. Enough hogs to support the proposed level of operation of the plant are available in the market area.

3. Can the proposed facility operate at a profit with the current market prices for beef and pork carcasses, the proposed level of output, and their investment necessary to establish the proposed facility?

Annual revenues from the sale of carcasses and offal would total $46,997,888; annual expenses for this level of production would total $45,038,237. The proposed facility could therefore operate at an annual net profit of $1,028,817 after taxes. These figures reflect average 1985 prices for animal inputs and carcasses.

4. Will the profit realized from the operation of the proposed facility justify the investment?

The rate of return (investment divided by net profit) on the capital requirements of the $5,784,282 for the proposed operation would be only 17.77 percent. Using the excess-present-value technique to compare the present value of the returns (net profit plus depreciation) that can be expected over the life of the proposed facility with the capital requirements for establishing the proposed venture, it is concluded that the proposed venture is economically feasible. The annual cash flows produce a return in excess of 15 percent.

Introduction

Purpose. The purpose of this study was to determine the economic feasibility of a "kill and chill" operation to be located in the city of Columbus, U.S.A. The study focused on the monetary feasibility of such an operation. This involved a preliminary assessment of markets for outputs and inputs of the proposed operation, projections of revenues and operating costs, and anlaysis of the anticipated return on investment.

Preliminary Assumptions. Several basic assumptions were made in developing the substantive materials that were analyzed in reaching the conclusions stated in the last section of the report. Because of the anticipated size of the operation, it was assumed that the plant would be federally inspected so that sales could be made in interstate commerce. Inspection is performed by the Meat Inspection Division of the Agricultural Research Service of the U.S. Department of Agriculture. All meat that moves in interstate commerce must be federally inspected.

Second, it was assumed that the proposed plant would concentrate on the market area represented by the three states. The market potential existing in these states and the anticipated size of the operation warrant such an assumption, as will be shown in the report.

The third assumption dealt with the exact nature of the operation. It was assumed that the plant would not be an integrated operation; that is, no feedlot operations would be maintained (other than that necessary to service working inventory) and no additional processing of slaughtered animals would take place. This assumption is based on information provided by the originators of the project and is vital in determining both costs and revenues to be derived from the proposed operation.

A final assumption was that the plant would operate at a predetermined level and would sell its entire output. Certain basic facilities are required to start such an operation. However, the use of such equipment may vary considerably as a result of seasonal variations in the availability of cattle and hogs and changes in the market for the products of the firm. This specified level of operation would entail slaughtering an average of three hundred cattle and three hundred hogs daily. Using a 250-workday calendar, this would result in an annual slaughter of 93,750 cattle and 93,750 hogs or a 187,500 annual slaughter. (The average output of such plants is 22,500 heads annually.) This production and sales level is vital to the analysis that follows. Operating at some other level of output than the one specified would substantially influence cost and revenues and would not be reflected in the analysis presented in this report.

It should also be pointed out that no attempt was made to analyze the managerial abilities of administrative personnel of the proposed plant. However, the profitability of any business operation depends on the possession of adequate managerial abilities by those personnel responsible for decision making within the organization.

Other assumptions are noted in the report where they are needed to facilitate the analysis.

Market Potential for Beef and Pork

Consumer Demand. Per capita consumption of beef in the United states is at an all-time high—116 pounds per year. This figure represents an increase of 6 pounds per capita in the seven-year period from 1975 to 1982. It is anticipated that consumption may reach 150 pounds per capita by 1989.

Pork consumption has also been increasing. Comparable figures are 63 pounds per capita in 1975, 67 pounds in 1982, and an anticipated 70 pounds per capita in 1989.

Tables B–3 and B–4 combined population figures for the market area—the three market area states—with per capita consumption values to yield total consumption of beef and pork, respectively. These values are then converted into the equivalent number of beef cows and hogs required to meet the consumption levels. These tables therefore show the number of beef cows and hogs consumed in the market area in 1985.

Table B–3
Estimated Market Area Beef Consumption for 1985

State	Population[a]	Per Capita Beef Consumption (pounds)[b]	Total Beef Consumption (pounds)	Beef Cow Equivalents (thousand head)[c]
State 1	4,402,000	116	510,630,000	945.6
State 2	4,667,000	116	541,370,000	1,002.5
State 3	2,836,875	116	329,080,000	609.4
	11,905,875		1,381,080,000	2,557.5

[a]"Annual Survey of Buying Power," *Sales Management*, August 1984.
[b]*The Farm Index*, U.S. Government Printing Office, Washington, D.C. 1985.
[c]Equivalent number of beef cows in thousands was computed using a 60 percent conversion factor and an average live weight of 900 pounds.

Table B–4
Estimated Market Area Pork Consumption for 1985

State	Population[a]	Per Capita Pork Consumption (pounds)[b]	Total Pork Consumption (pounds)	Hog Equivalents (thousand head)[c]
State 1	4,402,000	67	294,930,000	2,021.0
State 2	4,667,000	67	312,690,000	2,141.8
State 3	2,836,875	67	190,070,000	1,301.9
	11,905,875		797,680,000	5,464.7

[a]"Annual Survey of Buying Power," *Sales Management*, August 1984.
[b]*The Farm Index*, U.S. Government Printing Office, Washington, D.C. 1985.
[c]Equivalent number of hogs in thousands was computed using a 70 percent conversion factor and an average live weight of 208 pounds.

Market potential is defined as the maximum capacity of a market to purchase a specific type of offering in a specified time period. As shown in these two tables, consumption in the three-state area represents considerable market potential. The equivalent of over 2 million beef cows and 4 million hogs were consumed in this three-state area in 1985. These calculations are based on 1985 population and consumption estimates, and it should be noted that this is a conservative estimate of potential for the proposed plant. By the time the plant would begin operations, there would have been an increase in both population and average consumption of beef and pork.

Availability of Livestock Supplies. The proposed plant will probably be unable to secure adequate supplies of livestock from within the market area. In fact, a recent publication of the Research and Development Center in Columbus states that about 50 percent of all animals slaughtered in state 3 came from other states. Table B–5 shows the inventory of cattle and hogs in the market area in 1985.

Although the marketing of cattle and calves exceeds slaughter in the market area, most of the marketings are calves that are shipped to large feedlots in the West. The relatively large inventory of cattle and hogs is thus somewhat misleading. Since it is more economical to ship calves out West and feed them than to ship feed into the market area, the number of cattle available for slaughter is substantially less than the inventory would indicate. The same situation is generally true of hogs. This lack of slaughter animals in the market area can be seen more clearly in table B–6, which shows consumption and slaughter of cattle and hogs in the three-state area and the imports of animals needed to meet consumption levels. The equivalent of 1,846,750 beef cows and 2,373,750 hogs had to be improted into the three-state area to satisfy consumption needs in 1985.

Table B-5
Inventory of Cattle and Hogs in State 1, State 2, and State 3, 1985
(thousand head)

State	Cattle	Hogs
State 1	2,563	1,374
State 2	2,384	369
State 3	3,266	750
Totals	8,213	2,493

So far two basic facts have been established. The excess of consumption over slaughter in the market area establishes the existence of adequate potential for another slaughtering operation in the area. The large amount of beef imported into the area to satisfy market demands indicates that only a portion of the slaughter animals for the proposed plant could be supplied from within the area. The additional supplies (higher grades of animals) would have to be purchased outside the market area and shipped in at higher prices.

The excess of hog slaughter over consumption in the state indicates that supplies of hogs in the area would probably be sufficient to support the anticipated levels of production.

For purposes of this study, it was assumed that 20 percent of the beef slaughter animals would come from outside the market area.

Market Prices: Animal Inputs. One of the major factors determining the profitability of the proposed operation is the cost of raw materials—cattle and hogs. For purposes of analysis it was assumed that 20 percent of the cattle slaughtered by the plant would come from outside the market area. This assumption is based on the results of the analysis of the availability of animals previously discussed. At the proposed slaughter level of 93,750 cattle annually, this would mean that 18,750 slaughter animals would have to be procured from outside the market area and 75,000 from within the area. All the hogs slaughtered would be supplied from within the local area.

Even though the market for cattle and hogs was in such a state of uncertainty during the period of the study, it was felt that a reasonable approach to determining prices of inputs and outputs was taken. Although these prices may change substantially by the time actual operations begin, the margin of difference between the sets of prices should remain fairly constant.

The average price per hundredweight of beef cattle and hogs was $43.15 and $31.40, respectively, for the United States in 1985. The average price for cattle and hogs in state 3 was $40.55 and $32.00 for the same period.

Table B–6
Consumption, Slaughter, and Imports of Beef and Pork in State 1, State 2, and State 3, 1985
(thousand head)

State	Consumption (hundred head equivalent)	Slaughter[a]	Imports
Beef			
State 1	945.6	125.5	820.1
State 2	1,002.5	233.4	769.1
State 3	609.4	351.9	257.5
Totals	2,557.5	710.8	1,846.7
Pork			
State 1	2,021.0	1,194.4	826.6
State 2	2,141.8	290.3	1,851.5
State 3	1,301.9	1,606.3	– 304.4[c]
Totals	5,464.7	3,091.0	2,373.7

[a]Slaughter figures based on statistics in *Meat Animals*, U.S. Government Printing Office, Washington, D.C. April 1978, and estimates based on 1985 farm slaughter values.
[b]Slaughter of pork exceeded consumption in state 3.

In this study, the prices of $43.15 per hundredweight for beef cows from outside the area and $40.55 for those obtained within the area were used in computations. The hog price of $32.00 per hundredweight was used as the relevant hog input price. The difference in prices for beef inputs seems reasonable since the beef obtained outside the area would be higher grade animals.

There would also be a difference in transportation cost for animals obtained from outside the market area. Interviews with local truck operators and packing companies indicate that the rates for transportation of livestock are rising and that the methods used to compute rate are changing. Both will cause higher transportation costs in the future.

In computing transportation cost, a rate of $0.75 per hundredweight was used for animals acquired within the market area and $1.13 per hundredweight for animals brought in from outside the market area.

Cost of the Facility

Land Costs. The proposed slaughtering facility is to be located ten miles south of Columbus, U.S.A., on state 3 highway 7, 54 miles southeast of Baytown, 34 miles north of Saytown, 124 miles from New Cravens, and 43 miles from Tunis. This location places the proposed facility in an area that is relatively central to the major population concentration in the market area. This area also seems to have an adequate labor supply, is a major livestock-producing area, and has relatively low land values for industrial development of $2,439 per acre. Although this figure is somewhat higher than average land prices of

$935–$1,250 per acre for similar land around Columbus, it is considerably lower than the price of comparable land closer to major population areas and also lower than the appraised value of the land.

One hundred acres have been acquired by the corporation in exchange for stock. The total cost for this land is $243,900. Immediate space requirements for the plant facility, holding pens sufficient for at least 750 cattle and 750 hogs, parking lots and truck loading docks, water well sites, adequate expansion space, and sewage treatment facilities would not exceed fifteen acres. Thus one hundred acres is far in excess of the actual space requirement needs, and the expenditure for this amount substantially influences the rate of return on investment.

Conversely, there are several possible arguments in favor of initial acquisition of the total acreage. First, it provides the company with control of the environment in which the plant is located. This would enable the company to undertake future expansion into auxiliary processing operations or vertical integration of a feeding operation, should economic conditions warrant. Second, once the proposed plant is in operation, land adjacent to it would increase in value above present costs. Finally, any additional industrial development could be controlled by the company and would be an important fact in encouraging related industry, as well as becoming an additional source of revenue for the company. No attempt was made to judge the relative merits of these arguments.

Building Costs. Table B–7 shows the breakdown of building costs for the proposed facility. These cost estimates were provided by Martin Supplies, Inc., of Kansas City, Kansas. Although architectural specifications would be necessary for an accurate estimate of building costs, these estimates, at an

Table B–7
Breakdown of Building Costs

Work Area	Square Feet	Cost per Square Foot (average)	Cost
Basement	9,072	$37.50	$ 340,200
Kill floor	9,072	43.75	396,900
Beef chill cooler	2,560	43.75	112,000
Beef holding cooler	2,688	43.75	117,600
Hog cooler	1,600	43.75	70,000
Edible cooler	650	43.75	28,440
Cutting room	2,304	40.00	92,160
Dry storage room	480	37.50	18,000
Shipping dock	768	40.00	30,720
Office and restrooms	2,560	31.25	80,000
Totals	31,754	40.50	$1,286,020

Note: See table B–16 on page 154.

average of $40.50, seem to be somewhat high. Local estimates supplied by the originators of the project were approxiamtely $25 per square foot. It is assumed that the local estimate includes the special building characteristics required of a federally inspected slaughter facility. The local estimate is an average figure for the total building, with the processing areas at a higher rate and the non-processing areas at a much lower rate. Using local estimates, the cost of the plant facility would be $793,850.

The accuracy of the estimate of building costs will substantially influence the amount of capital required to initiate the project. A variance of only a dollar per square foot would amount to a $40,500 error. Therefore, without architectural plans and a firm bid from a local contractor, it must be assumed that the estimate provided by Martin Supplies is the best current estimate available, since it reflects the judgment of a firm experienced in the construction of slaughtering facilities. It is assumed that these figures include allowances for parking and holding pens sufficient for 750 cattle and 750 hogs, a two-day supply at the state level of output. According to federal regulations, holding pens must be paved with curbs. Parking areas must also be hard-surfaced to keep airborne particles to an acceptable level. It is assumed that the local estimates do not include these features. Also, according to information supplied by the originators of the project, the Martin estimates include an additional 15 percent to offset possible increases in building materials and labor costs before the facility can be built. This would account for $193,131 of the discrepancy between the two estimates. The remaining $300,568 difference in estimates is an amount in excess of the possible costs of holding pens and parking facilities. It may reflect the differences in construction labor costs between Kansas City and Columbus. Verifying the accuracy of these estimates is beyond the scope of this investigation and perhaps impossible without architectural plans, which are not available. Therefore, the Martin estimates will be used in the financial and economic analysis as the best current estimate of the complete facility, including building, holding pens, and parking and loading facilities.

Table B–8 shows other building costs estimates supplied by Martin Supplies Inc. Since the land required has no existing water and sewage treatment

Table B–8
Other Building Costs

Purpose	Cost
Site preparation	$ 31,250
Sewer system	62,500
Engineering	62,500
Road work	37,500
Total	$193,750

Note: See table B–16 on page 154.

facilities adequate to handle the needs of the proposed slaughtering facility, these costs are shown here. Again, these figures are 15 percent above current costs to offset effects of inflation before actual construction can be completed. This is $29,065 in excess of present costs.

Federal regulations and practical considerations require that access roads in the vicinity of the plant be hard-surfaced. Costs for drilling two 900-foot water wells and constructing a tank to meet the needs of the proposed facility of 30,000 gallons per hour are not included because of the lack of available data.

Equipment Costs. Total equipment costs f.o.b. Martin Supplies, Inc., Kansas City, Kansas, are $1,036,821. It is assumed that the equipment listed and the prices quoted are in competition with industry rates and that the equipment is adequate for the type of operation and the proposed level of output of the facility. Transportation of equipment to the plant site and installation are not included in these figures. Average industry transportation costs are 5 percent of sales price, and installation costs are 17 percent of sales price. Again, equipment prices are 15 percent above current prices to offset any future price increases before the plant can be completed. For the purposes of this report, the 15 percent will be used to partially offset transportation and installation charges. Should price increases occur before the plant is constructed, it is possible that total costs for equipment, installation, and transportation to the plant site would be considerably higher than the total shown here.

All fixed-cost estimates supplied by Martin Supplies, Inc., are 15 percent above current costs, a total of $222,195. In addition, the difference between cost estimates of the building from Martin and those from local contractors is $443,699. This would provide $665,895 to cover construction of holding pens, water supply, transportation, installation of equipment, architectural fees, and parking areas. Assuming a certain amount of inaccuracy in the estimates of local contractors without firm bids or architectural specifications, it is probably that Martin's cost estimates are sufficiently inflated to cover the nonspecific items mentioned and retain a comfortable cushion for possible future price increases. The breakdown of cost estimates supplied by Martin is considered quite unrealistic in many instances, but the overall cost estimate for the facility and equipment is the highest possible cost assuming that the facility could be built for considerably less than these estimates. This would substantially reduce the capital investment and also affect estimates of the rate of ROI. Table B–9 summarizes the total costs of the facility.

Working Capital Requirements. The meat and processing industry requires a large investment in working capital. Most of this working capital is used to finance the large inventories of slaughter animals. Recent financial records of two firms in the meat industry revealed a net working capital of about 10 percent of sales; initial working capital requirements would not be quite this large.

Table B–9
Summary of Facility Costs

Source	Cost
Land	$ 243,875
Building	1,287,549
Other building costs	193,750
Equipment	1,036,821
Total	$2,761,995

It will be shown later on that total yearly expenses of operations are estimated to be $36,266,839. The assumption that initial working capital requirements are equal to one month's expenses yields a requirement of $3,022,237. This seems to be a reasonable amount considering the methods of payment and factoring services available in the industry.

For purposes of this study, a $3,022,237 investment in working capital was assumed to be the appropriate capital needed to begin operations. This figure is about 8 percent of the anticipated sales revenue. Since the investment in building, land, and equipment totals $2,761,995, the total capital requirements will be $5,784,232. Thus the proposed venture would be one of the largest undertaken in the state in recent years.

Revenues, Expenses, and Return on Investment

Revenues. The revenue derived from operations will come from two sources: (1) sales of the carcasses of the slaughtered animals and (2) sales of by-products of the slaughtering operation. As previously pointed out, there will be no processing of hogs into pork products such as bacon, sausage, and the like in the proposed operation. Thus revenue will come basically from carcass sales and sales of the hides and offal of the slaughtered animals. Output of the plant will be sold primarily to other meat wholesalers and processors. Table B–10 shows the sales revenues from the output of the operation.

Beef Sales Revenues. The average wholesale price of a beef carcass in 1985 was $67.34 per hundredweight. The estimated average price for hides and offal of cattle was $5.23 per hundred pounds live weight. Thus a 900-pound slaughter animal would yield about $364 in carcass sales (5.4 hundredweight [cut] times $67.34) and $47 in hide and offal revenue (9 hundredweight times $5.23).

Total revenue for the 75,000 annual cattle slaughtered would amount to $38,503,688—$34,090,875 in carcass revenues and $4,412,813 in revenues from the hides and offal.

Table B–10
Sales Revenues by Product Type

Product Type	Number of Hundredweights of Each Product Produced[a]	Sales Price per Hundredweight[b]	Total Revenues by Product Type
Beef			
Carcass	506,250	$67.34	$34,090,875
Hides and offal	843,750	5.23	4,412,813
Total revenue—beef			$38,503,688
Pork			
Carcass	195,000[c]	$37.85[e]	$ 7,380,750
Hides and offal	195,000[d]	5.71[e]	1,113,450
Total revenue—pork			$ 8,494,200
Total revenue—beef and pork			$46,997,888

[a]Based on 93,750 cattle and 93,750 hogs slaughtered at an average live weight of 900 and 208 pounds, respectively. Conversion rates of 60 and 70 percent were used in completing the number of hundredweights of each product type.

[b]Based on average prices per hundredweight of carcasses, hides, and offal for 1985.

[c]Dressed weight for cattle and live weight for hogs.

[d]Live weight—prices for offal and hides are reported in U.S. Department of Agiculture publications in terms of estimates per hundredweight of live animals.

[e]Estimated from industry revenue percentages for carcasses and by-products.

Pork Sales Revenues. The average wholesale value of pork, including by-products, was $43.56 per 100 pounds live weight in 1985. Since pork is usually processed into bacon, sausage, hams, and the like before being sold to retailers, the wholesale *value* of pork was used instead of the wholesale *price*. The difference between the wholesale value and the wholesale price should reflect the additional processing cost or value added by processing.

Pork by-products, including lard, would yield approximately $5.68 per hundredweight. Carcass value would average about $37.85 per hundredweight. Total revenue from hog slaughter would amount to $8,494,200–$7,380,750 in carcass revenues and $1,113,450 in revenues from by-products. The combined revenues for the proposed plant would be approximately $46,997,888 in 1985 prices.

Operating Expenses. Four major categories of expense are discussed in this section: (1) cost of animal inputs, (2) wages and salaries, (3) other employee expenses, and (4) other operating expenses.

Cost of Animal Inputs. One of the major operating costs for the proposed plant will be the cost of animal inputs. Table B–11 shows the breakdown of the cost of these inputs. To derive the total cost of each input type, the following basic formula was used:

Table B–11
Cost of Animal Inputs

Inputs	Number of Animals[a]	Price per 100 Pounds[b]	Total Cost
Cattle			
Within market area	75,000	$41.28	$27,864,000
Outside market area	18,750	44.28	7,472,300
Hogs	93,750	32.75	6,386,300
Totals	187,500		$41,722,600

[a]Based on the assumption of a 93,750 annual cattle slaughter and 20 percent obtained outside the market area. Average slaughter weights of 900 pounds and 208 pounds were used for cattle and hogs, respectively.
[b]Prices include transportation costs of $0.75/hundredweight within the area and $1.13/hundredweight outside the area.

Total cost of the input = Number of animals × (average slaughter weight ÷ 100) × average price per hundredweight + transportation per hundredweight × total hundredweight of animals.

For the 75,000 cattle supplied through market area sources, a price of $40.53 per hundredweight and a transportation rate of $0.75 were used. A price of $43.15 and a transportation rate of $1.13 were used for the 18,750 cattle to be procured from outside the area. These calculations yielded a total cost of cattle inputs of $35,336,300—$27,864,000 for cattle procured in the area and $7,472,300 for animals outside the area.

For hogs, a price of $32.00 and a transportation rate of $0.75 were used in calculations. This yielded a total cost of hog inputs of $6,386,300 of the 93,750 annual slaughter. The combined cost of animal inputs totaled $41,722,600.

Wages and Salaries. This plant has a total of 127 personnel. Of this total, 115 are production or auxiliary personnel, with 86 of these employees classified as unskilled and 29 as skilled. Information supplied by the U.S. Employment Security Division estimates the industry average wages for jobs classified as unskilled at $4.05 per hour and for skilled workers at $4.80. Total costs per year for production workers for fifty forty-hour weeks are $690,375.

Table B–12 shows the office and administrative personnel and yearly salaries for each. Salaries of management personnel quoted are for personnel experienced in the slaughter industry. Total yearly salaries for office and administrative staff are $193,500. Total yearly wages and salaries for all personnel are $883,875.

Other Employee Expenses. Other expenses of the proposed operation directly related to personnel are insurance and hospitalization; employment security taxes; social security taxes; vacation, holidays, and sick leave; and retirement.

Table B–12
Salary Schedule for Administrative and Office Personnel

Production Manager	$ 34,250 (includes $1,250 expenses)
Plant manager	$ 38,750 (includes $1,250 expenses)
Production manager	25,000
Sales manager	21,250 (includes $1,250 expenses)
Personnel manager	15,000
Receptionist	6,000
Office workers (6)	38,250
Accountant	15,000
Total	$193,500

The company's expense for an insurance and hospitalization program would be approximately $26,670. This is based on estimates supplied by a local insurance representative who quoted an industry average of $17.50 per employee. This figure includes average life insurance and hospitalization benefits for the local area. For all plant personnel, monthly premiums would total $2,222.50.

Employment security taxes vary with the claim record of the employer, but the industry average for the local area is 2.5 percent of total wages and salaries. Assuming a normal employment pattern, total employment security taxes would be $22,097.

Social security taxes are figured at the rate of 6.85 percent of the first $12,000 in earnings. Using the average wage figures for production and auxiliary personnel, all of the total wages of $690,375 would be subject to social security taxes. Salaries of $119,250 for office and administrative personnel would be subject to social security taxes. Thus total employer's contribution for social security would be $55,459.

Paid vacation, holidays, and sick leave are figured at ten working days. Total costs would be $27,615. Since salaried personnel are paid on a monthly basis, this figure includes only the additional expenses for wage employees.

It is assumed that a company of this size will have a retirement program for its employees. Because a retirement plan was not formulated by the originators of the project, the minimal contribution by the employer of such a program is taken as equal to social security taxes. This is below the industry average; however, since state 3 corporations do not typically have retirement programs, it is considered adequate. Table B–13 summarizes expenses for wages, salaries, and employee benefits.

Other Expenses. In addition to the operation expenses previously estimated, several other categories of expenses should be identified and enumerated. As was shown earlier, the total investment required in the proposed operation would be about $5,784,250. Assuming all authorized stock is sold and $4,250,000

Table B–13
Total Annual Employee Expense Schedule

Item	Cost
Wages and salaries	
Production and Auxiliary Personnel	$690,375
Administrative and Office Personnel	193,500
Employee benefits	
Insurance and hospitalization	26,670
Employment security taxes	22,097
Social security taxes	55,459
Vacation, holidays, and sick leave	27,615
Retirement	55,459
Total Expenses	$1,071,175

(value of authorized stock issue minus stock sales commissions and other fees) is available for financing the investment, an additional $1,534,250 would have to be secured through debt financing. The originators of the project plan to apply for an FHA-secured loan for the additional finances needed to begin operations. If their application is accepted, an 8.25 percent loan could be obtained.

Based on a repayment period of twenty-five years and an 8.25 percent interest rate, the debt retirement and interest schedule is shown in table B–14. Total interest charges over the life the loan would be $1,734,711, for an average interest expense of $69,388.

The investment in equipment and building developed in the previous section was $2,761,995: $1,036,821 for the equipment and $1,725,174 for the building. Assuming the equipment would be depreciated over an eight-year period and the building over a twenty-five-year period, the annual depreciation expense would total $267,490.

The current millage for property taxes in Stevens County is 61 mills, and assessed values are about 15 percent of market values. Using this tax rate and structure, the annual property tax for the proposed plant would be $27,668.

The expense for supplies and containers averages about 2.1 percent of total sales. Since there will be no processing of slaughtered animals, a figure of 1 percent of sales was used for the plant. this would be about $469,979 a year. All other expenses are estimated at 3 percent of sales, the industry average for regional meat packers. This would be $1,409,937 in the proposed operation on an annual basis. This includes expenses for power, fuel, legal and audit charges, sales expenses, bad debt expense, and so on.

Pro Forma Income Statement. Previous sections set forth the results of the analysis of anticipated revenues and expenses for the proposed venture. These results have been used to develop the pro forma income statement shown in table B–15. Expenses, including the cost of animal inputs, totaled $45,038,237.

Table B–14
Debt Retirements and Interest Schedule

Year	Principal	Annual Interest Charge	End of year Payment
1	$1,534,250	$134,247	$60,970
2	1,463,280	128,037	60,970
3	1,402,310	122,702	60,970
4	1,341,340	117,367	60,970
5	1,280,370	112,032	60,970
6	1,219,400	106,698	60,970
7	1,158,430	101,363	60,970
8	1,097,460	96,028	60,970
9	1,036,490	90,693	60,970
10	975,520	85,358	60,970
11	914,550	80,023	60,970
12	853,580	74,688	60,970
13	792,610	69,353	60,970
14	731,640	64,019	60,970
15	670,670	58,684	60,970
16	609,700	53,349	60,970
17	548,730	48,014	60,970
18	487,760	42,679	60,970
19	426,790	37,344	60,970
20	365,820	32,009	60,970
21	304,850	26,674	60,970
22	243,880	21,340	60,970
23	183,910	16,005	60,970
24	121,940	10,670	60,970
25	60,970	5,335	60,970

This amount was subtracted from total sales revenue to determine profits before taxes. Federal and state corporate income taxes were then subtracted to determine the net profits from operations: $1,028,817.

Present-Value Analysis and Return on Investment. The returns from an investment are defined for decision-making purposes as the net inflows of cash expected from a project. In the case of the proposed venture, this would be equal to the net profit after taxes plus depreciation: $1,296,307. The total capital requirements for the plant were computed to be $5,784,282. The weighted average life of the investment would be eighteen years.

Excess present value is a common technique used to determine whether the returns from an investment justify the capital requirements of the investment. The present value of the returns over the life of the investment are equal to $7,943,769 ($1,296,307 × 6.128 at a 15 percent minimum acceptable rate of return). Since the present value of the returns ($7,943,769) is greater than the project's capital requirements ($5,784,282), the proposed venture is economically feasible.

Table B–15
Pro Forma Income Statement

Sales		$46,997,888
Cost of inputs		41,722,600
Gross margin		$ 5,275,288
Expenses	$ 883,875	
Salaries and wages		
Other employee expenses:		
Insurance	26,670	
Retirement	55,459	
Vacation and sick leave	27,615	
Social security taxes	55,459	
Employment security taxes	22,097	
Other expenses		
Depreciation	267,490	
Interest	69,388	
Property taxes	27,668	
Supplies	469,979	
All other expenses	1,409,937	
Total expenses		$ 3,315,637
Profit before income tax		$ 1,959,651
Corporate income taxes (federal and state)		$ – 930,834
Net profit after taxes		$ 1,028,817

The rate of return on investment is computed by dividing net profit after taxes by the total investment. The rate of return for the proposed operation is equal to 17.77 percent. Rate of return does not consider net cash inflows generated by a project, since it is computed using net profits. The net profit figure of $1,028,817 represents only a 2.19 percent return on sales. This return on sales reflects the low overall profitability of the meat industry.

Conclusions

This study was conducted within the framework of the assumptions stated in the first four sections, and the conclusions reached on the basis of this study are tenable only within the framework of these assumptions. For example, it was assumed that the level of output would be 187,500 slaughtered animals annually. If, in fact, a higher level of production could be achieved, net profit should be increased. On the other hand, a lower level of output should decrease net profits.

Based on the analysis of ROI and the present value of the cash flows generated by the investment, the plant is economically feasible. The present value of cash flows over the life of the investment was greater than the investment required to begin operations. Although net profits as a percentage of sales are low, the ROI was estimated at 17.77 percent.

Note that many of the figures used in this study were estimates based on projections of historical data collected specifically for this study. There is no way to determine the reliability of such estimates; however, these figures are the best estimates available.

Table B–16 provides a breakdown of the building cost estimates.

Table B–16
Rollco Packing Company: Breakdown of Building Cost Estimates

		Square Feet	Cost per Square Foot	Cost
Basement	72 × 126	9,072	$37.50	$ 340,200.00
Kill floor	72 × 126	9,072	43.75	396,900.00
Beef chill cooler	40 × 64	2,560	43.75	112,000.00
Beef holder cooler	42 × 64	2,688	43.75	117,600.00
Hog cooler	32 × 50	1,600	43.75	70,000.00
Edible cooler	13 × 50	650	43.75	28,440.00
Cutting room	48 × 48	2,304	40.00	92,160.00
Dry storage room	12 × 40	480	37.50	18,000.00
Shipping dock	64 × 12	768	40.00	30,720.00
Office and restrooms	80 × 32	2,560	31.25	80,000.00
Building cost				$1,286,020.00
Equipment cost				1,036,821.00
Site preparation				31,250.00
Sewer system				62,500.00
Engineering				62,500.00
Road work				37,500.00
Preliminary total estimate of project				$2,516,591.00

Market Opportunity Analysis:
Travel-Trailer Park

Prepared by:
Triad Marketing Research Group
P.O. Box 700895
Tulsa, OK 74170
(918) 493-3787

Tulsa, Oklahoma
December, 1986

The purpose of this study is twofold:

1. To develop the background, criteria, and process for selecting a suitable location for a medium-sized travel-trailer park in the Northwest Madison region.
2. To set forth basic facts, economic projections, demand analysis, competition analysis, social considerations, governmental factors, conclusions, and recommendations relative to the development of a travel-trailer or recreational-vehicle park.

The study focuses on the economic feasibility of investing and managing a travel-trailer park with a maximum initial development cost in the range of $200,000–$250,000.

The specific objectives of the study are as follows:

1. To evaluate past national and regional trends in the recreational-vehicle and outdoor recreation industries.
2. To determine and analyze those factors that have characterized the growth and development of travel trailer parks.
3. To determine present and potential market and demand patterns.
4. To evaluate competition.
5. To formulate plans, objectives, and goals for developing, marketing, and managing a travel-trailer park.
6. To make financial projections.
7. To evaluate the returns on the proposed investment.

Scope and Limitations

No attempt was made to analyze the managerial abilities of administrative personnel of the proposed operation. However, the profitability of any business depends on the possession of adequate managerial skills by those personnel responsible for decision making within the organization.

The study highlights conclusions and recommendations, provides an overview of the tourism and recreation market in general and in Northwest Madison in particular, and then proceeds to a competitive analysis of existing private facilities and the resulting most viable marketing strategy. The study concludes with a site and location analysis, a financial feasibility analysis, and an analysis of an existing park for sale.

Summary of Conclusions and Recommendations

Based on the results of the analysis undertaken in this study, the following conclusions have been drawn:

Locate near a population center—this will be the future trend. Also, this is advantageous if gasoline prices cause campers to make shorter trips in the future.

Locate on the south or west shoreline of Grand Lake, near a dominant recreation attraction or close to an existing destination-type park with a high level of amenities.

Consider investment in a combination travel-trailer or recreational-vehicle (RV) and mobile-home (MH) park, but locate to maximize the recreation-vehicle aspect of the development.

A park having many amenities has the lowest risk, and the trend is definitely toward destination-type parks. Of course, this type of park requires a higher investment.

The quality of the park's development and the extent of its improvements depend on local demand, the amount of rent that can be collected, and the amenities the competition is offering. Analysis of the market suggests that the greatest need relative to competition is to:

1. Develop a new park (or purchase and improve an existing park) that offers amenities at the high end of the range (similar to Safari, located on Highway 10).

2. Price rental space just below the market, at $7.50 per unit (including all amenities except extra people).

3. Offer the following amenities: fishing, boating, grocery store, laundry, restrooms, vending machines, group shelter, picnic area, playground, children's facilities, recreation building, and all hookups.

4. Develop a park that has somewhere between 40 spaces and 100 spaces.

Marketing strategy should include:

1. Price slightly below the high-amenity parks

2. Heavy promotional activities, especially on signs from major highways

3. Strong consumer orientation to encourage repeat business

Management strategy should include:

1. A professional approach to managing the business through setting income and occupancy goals, developing sound policies for resident behavior in and about the premises, and dealing effectively with the local community

2. An aggressive approach to improving occupancy levels by appropriate marketing

3. An effective cost-control system to minimize expenses, and sound inventory management (store goods)

4. Effective skills to handle resident complaints and troublemakers—particularly the noise problem

External Analysis: Tourism and Recreation—
An Industry Overview

The concept of a travel-trailer park brings us to consideration of the tourism and recreation industries, of which it is a part. This section of the report highlights current trends in tourism and recreation both at a national-state level and, specifically, in Northwest Madison.

One basic question in light of both energy costs and inflation is the future of both tourism and recreation. Tourism expenditures are influenced by both inflation and energy problems, recreational expenditures mainly by inflation. All available evidence suggests that the problems that beset these industries in the early 1970s have not led to the predicted sluggishness. The availability of gasoline at relatively stable prices and increases in personal income have both worked to offset a decline in these industries.

There are also indications that a growing proportion of families consider travel and vacation a necessity rather than a luxury. Responses to energy shortages and inflation are more likely to be shorter, less expensive trips than a cancellation of planned activities.

Another strong indication of current strength is the strong showing of recreational vehicles in terms of total shipments. Most of the increase has been in motor homes and travel trailers, which accounted for about 60 percent of total recreational vehicle shipments in 1980.

These facts lead to an assumption of continued growth in travel and recreational activities, both in general and specifically in Northwest Madison.

Tourism and Recreation: Northwest Madison

The state of Madison in general and Northwest Madison in particular have developed and supported a great deal of tourist and recreation-oriented attractions in the last decade. The development of the Grand Dam and Reservoir gave impetus to more rapid development of the area.

Northwest Madison moved from the second-ranking area for overnight visitors in 1980 to the top-ranked area in 1982, 1984, and 1986. Of the total of 24,107,500 overnight visitors to Madison in 1986, about 22 percent were in Northwest Madison (see table B–17). Jefferson County attracts the greatest

Table B–17
Overnight Visitors to Northwest Madison, 1986

County	Visitors	State Share
Jefferson	2,543,340	10.55%
Carrollton	2,143,155	8,89%
Madisonville	26,515	0.11%
Webster	605,100	2.51%
Totals	5,318,110	22.06%

Sources: *Tourism in Madison*, Madison State Publishing, 1986.

number of overnight visitors. Although Webster County is far behind, it leads the entire Northwest Madison region as the economic and population center. Thus Webster County can be a source of weekend business during the slow seasons.

Overnight Campers. Of specific importance to the feasibility of the travel-trailer facility is the number of overnight campers. As shown in table B–18 for the state, overnight campers accounted for about 7.2 percent of the overnight visitors in 1986. More pertinent to this study is the number of group nights as shown in table B–19. That is the total number of parties (three to four people) times the number of nights stayed in a particular area. These calculations are as follows for the state as a whole and then estimated for Northwest Madison.

Tables B–18 and B–19 together show that in 1986, for example, 97,904 camping parties came to Northwest Madison, stayed an average of 7.6 days, and demanded 3,641,594 RV campsites and 137,653 tent campsites. The two explicit assumptions in these calculations are that Northwest Madison's share of campers is at least equal to its share of all overnight visitors, and that the percentages of campers by type are the same in Northwest Madison as for the state as a whole.

Data supplied by the Corps of Engineers reveal that Grand Lake is one of the most popular resort areas in the state by visitation counts and that it has also experienced rapid growth in the last nine years. Specific data on Grand Lake show that Hickory Creek and Bill's Creek are the two most popular park areas on Grand Lake. Both have experienced increased use in the last five years.

Northwest Madison Economic Development. An important factor in the feasibility of any business is the health of the environment in which the firm must operate. This section presents data on per capita income and population for the area.

Table B–20 shows a substantial growth in population and per capita income in the four-county area, especially in Jefferson and Webster Counties. In these two counties, a 70 percent increase in population and almost a 200 percent increase in average household effective buying income occurred between

Table B–18
Camping Activity in Madison, 1982–1986

	1982	1984	1986
Overnight campers	$ 1,788,700	$ 1,885,470	$ 1,730,900
Parties	506,030	496,175	443,810
Average stay (nights)	7.4	6.8	7.6
Persons per party	3.6	3.8	3.9
Person-night	13,480,640	12,821,160	13,154,530
Spent per party-night	$31.45	$33.87	$35.97
Annual economic impact	$117,768,360	$114,277,040	$121,325,220
Percentage by category			
Truck-camp	33.5%	32.0%	32.5%
RV-camp	49.6%	50.0%	49.0%
Tent-camp	16.9%	18.0%	18.5%
Total	100.0%	100.0%	100.0%
Trip-nights	3,744,622	3,373,990	3,372,956

Source: *Tourism in Madison*, Madison State Publishing 1986 edition, p. 6.

Note: Camping statistics are based on state park superintendent monthly reports, private camp-ground owner surveys, and U.S. Army Corps of Engineers and National Forest Service monthly reports. Camper expenditures are based on estimates of the national 3M Company.

1970 and estimates for 1986. Population projections for Jefferson and Webster counties are 179,380 for 1988 and 197,074 for 1993. This would reflect a 16 percent increase in population for the two-county area between 1986 and 1993 estimates. Clearly, this will be one of the major growth areas in Madison during the next decade.

Thus a good basis for future development and expansion of the area has been established, and there is a very favorable political and resident attitude toward progress.

Competitive Analysis

Three basic marketing strategies are used by private trailer park facilities. One strategy is aimed at the overnight or "pass-through" market. These parks are designed to appeal to travelers en route to some predetermined destination or to those who are in a location for a short (one- to three-day) period. These parks are usually near major highways and offer only a few amenities.

A second strategy is aimed at those travelers who are planning an extended stay (four to seven days) in a particular area—usually a resort or other major tourist attraction. Although the trailer park contains few amenities, it is located very close to, if not adjacent to, such amenities. For example, a park might be located next to a Corps of Engineers recreation area on a lake.

In a third strategy, also aimed at the extended traveler, the park itself offers all or most of the amenities and may or may not be located close to other amenities. The park itself thus becomes the attraction, offering facilities and services geared to guests who will remain in the area for a few days.

Table B–19
Camper Party Nights: State and Region

	State			Region[a]		
	1982	1984	1986	1982	1984	1986
Parties	506,030	496,175	443,810	103,129	109,010	97,904
Average stay	7.4	6.8	7.6	7.4	6.8	7.6
Party nights	3,744,622	3,373,990	3,372,956	763,155	741,268	744,070

[a]These figures are conservative for Northwest Madison, since the use of camping facilities would not be proportional to total visitors in an area. Northwest Madison has a higher than proportional demand for this type of facility.

All three strategies are being used in the region of Madison under consideration. The major competitors in the Webster County–Jefferson County area are shown in table B–21.

Table B–21, which shows the facilities offered by different competitors, clearly demonstrates the differences in services offered in this area. Jellystone Park is by far the most complete; using the concept of a resort in itself, it offers a full range of services. KOA and Safari use the same strategy, but with fewer amenities. KOA's location on Highway 12 also appeals to overnighters. The Safari unit is being expanded at present.

Jim Bob's Trailer Park uses the strategy of not providing amenities but being located close to them. It is within 200 yards of the Corps of Engineers Hickory Creek Recreational Area. Although it offers nothing more than a place to park a travel trailer, a store, boats, bait, picnic tables, and so on are all available within 500 yards of the park. A couple of mobile home parks offer overnight hookups, but they cater strictly to overnighters as well as the overflow from the other RV parks.

A new proposed park located only 100 yards off Highway 78 north of Lucedale is planned and is awaiting a zoning decision. Judging from the location and the amount of land used in development, it would appear to be aimed at the pass-through or short-stay market.

Table B–20
Northwest Madison Population and Income Statistics

County	Population				Medium Effective Buying Income per Household			
	1970[a]	1980[a]	1984[a]	1986[b]	1970[b]	1980[b]	1984[b]	1986
Jefferson	40,009	55,524	65,670	67,320	$ 4,495	$ 7,983	$ 9,526	$13,346
Carrollton	12,412	13,531	15,400	16,280	4,079	6,529	7,126	9,739
Madisonville	9,975	10,398	11,110	11,880	4,236	5,774	6,249	8,857
Webster	61,376	85,107	98,340	102,410	5,157	10,047	10,586	14,362

Sources:
[a]*State and County Economic Data for Madison*, Industrial Research and Extension Center, University of Madison.
[b]Survey of Buying Power, *Sales Management Magazine*, June–August 1971, 1981, 1984, 1986.

Table B–21
RV Trailer Parks by Type of Amenities

RV Trailer Park	Coffee Snack Bar	Group Shelter	Rest-rooms	Laundry Room	Swimming Pool	Sanitary Dump	Showers	Picnic Tables
KOA (Highway 12)	X		X	X	X	X	X	X
Jellystone Park (highway 80)	X	X	X	X	X	X	X	X
Safari (Highway 10) (County 30)	X		X	X	X	X	X	
Jim Bob's Trailer Park (Hickory Creek Recreation Area)					X			
Karl's Mobile Home Park (Highway 78, Lucedale)					X			X

[a]Currently expanding—will double capacity
[b]Approximate.

The RV park industry offers special opportunities today for investment in destination-type parks. The overnight RV park is, in general, a poor investment. In coming years, major oil companies will take over this business. Their approach makes private investment in overnight spaces impractical. We have learned that the oil companies have a long-term plan to open overnight stops in conjunction with service stations. Facilities will be spartan and rates very low. Each station will have only ten to fifty spaces; their goal is more service station business. Service station personnel will operate the parks, so there will be little or no management expense. Many such parks are already in operation.

Thus real opportunities in the RV park business are destination parks. These parks are usually close to major population centers (no more than two to four hours driving time away) and offer urban RV owners a chance for fun on weekends and on vacations away from home. Such parks demand a major financial commitment because they require many activities to keep guests busy. Typical activities offered at such facilities are swimming; fishing; boating; golf (including miniature golf); children's playgrounds; horseback riding; snowmobiling; skiing; separate recreational buildings for adults, teenagers, and children; tennis; ping-pong; shuffleboard; horseshoes; archery; hayrides; picnic areas; hiking and bicycle trails; restaurants and bars; a general store; laundries; movies; and so on. Most important are planned recreation programs for children, teenagers, and adults. Such parks earn about half their revenue from fees other than those for space. The goal is fun for everyone, so visitors will stay longer and return frequently.

Rec. Room	Boats	Teen Hut	Planned Activities	All Hook-Ups	Tennis Courts	Barbeque Grill	Ten Area	Play ground	Number of Units
X				X			X	X	60
X	X	X	X	X	X	X	X		60
	X				X	X			24[a]
	X								39
									10[b]

A second category of destination parks require less investment in facilities but usually have high land costs. Located near major attractions such as a Disneyland, these parks attract visitors by the availability of fun and sightseeing activities outside the park.

RV park rates are rising rapidly, but RV travel still represents a big saving over other modes of travel. The increase is due to rising costs, of course, but even more to the fact that RV buyers are affluent and will pay more for more deluxe park facilities. The RV park developer should ignore the overnight park strategy, although destination parks do accept overnight visitors. Although the rate of return for a successful RV investment is higher than for a mobile-home park, the risk is also much higher. Feasibility studies for RV parks are much more subject to error, whereas such studies for mobile home parks are almost fool proof. One problem with RV park investments is that mortgage money is more difficult to obtain for them than for mobile home parks. The financial community knows of the long successful record for MH parks, but RV parks are much newer and have no well-established financial record.

Developing a Viable Marketing Strategy

One consistent observation of private nonfranchised trailer parks is the lack of an effective marketing program. This section will outline the marketing activities that should be a part of the overall management of any park.

Target Market. Every attempt should be made to identify potential customers of the services offered by the RV park. This market, like all others, includes several segments:

1. *Cross-country travelers:* Travelers en route to a predetermined destination, looking strictly for overnight hookups
2. *Cross-country travelers:* Travelers en route to a specific area of the country, but with no definite destination in mind, who are looking for some overnight and some short-stay (two- to four-day) accommodations
3. *Local area residents:* Usually weekenders on short trips with a predetermined destination—perhaps a tourist attraction such as a horse show or a lake recreation area—in mind, who mostly want overnight hookups but also need some short-stay accommodations
4. *RV clubs, large multiunit family groups, sports spectators, and the like:* These may be local area residents or nonlocal residents, depending on the nature of the group involved. They may want only overnight accommodations for a short stay.

The marketing mix—location, amenities, price, promotion, and so on—developed should be put together with specific groups in mind. For example, a strictly overnight park would be located close to a major highway, offer few amenities, and not require a park there. The following diagram shows some of the possible positions available for a new park attempting to fit in with existing offerings.

Low Amenities				*High Amenities*
Karl's Mobile Home Park	Jim Bob's Travel Trailer Park	KOA	Safari	Yogi Bear's Park

The current trend in travel trailer parks is in the direction of the high-amenity Yogi Bear Park concept. These parks appeal to the extended-stay (five to seven days) market, with a complete array of amenities from laundry rooms to planned activities for children. At the other end of the scale is the mobile home park that has a few sites for travel trailers and offers no specific amenities for the traveler.

Placement somewhere close to the Safari–Yogi Bear end of the spectrum with high amenities appears to be the best fit given the nature of demand and competition. Especially if a location close to a major highway is selected, a broader appeal can be developed to attract the overnight or short-stay groups.

Product Place. Offer a fairly accessible location, close to big attractions and metropolitan areas with a fully developed park theme. The park theme includes the name of the park, its architecture style, landscaping, and promotion. This requires more creative thinking than anything else (including money). For example, if a western theme is chosen, then the name of the park should be western in nature, as should landscaping, names of streets or driveways, appearance of the store, and so on. This gives the whole park a personality and excitement found in the more progressive parks.

Probably 40 to 100 sites either constructed or at least available for development will be most feasible. All hookups should be provided with other amenities such as a swimming pool, laundry, bath area, store, covered shelter, and picnic tables.

Price. The price charged should reflect three things: competition, amenities offered, and costs associated with serving a guest. More amenities mean a higher price; people understand and accept this. A current price structure reflecting these factors would be as follows:

All hookups (two people)	$7.50
Water and electricity	7.00
No hookups	5.50
Charge for each additional person	0.50
Air conditioner or heater	1.00

This price structure reflects current competitive price for a park with several amenities, but also charges those that use a service more than nonusers. Basic level of prices reflects the number of amenities offered. Jim Bob's Trailer Park currently offers no amenities and charges a flat rate of $4.50 a night.

Promotion. Travelers, unless they have been at the park before, don't know where it is located, what it offers, or how to get to the park. Promotion must tell them all this. Highway signs with additional arrow signs to the park location are a must. Listings in national travel guides are important since these guides are used extensively by travelers.

Any list of numbers of a travel-trailer club or group can bring in business. Aggressive selling and promotion will produce good results, since few operators actively seek out and sell to new customers. Every customer who stays is a potential for another stay, as well as a potential source of names and word-of-mouth advertising for the park. Good service will bring in new customers and bring back old customers. Poor service, obviously, will have the opposite effect.

Site and Location Analysis

A thorough analysis of Northwest Madison suggests that the Grand Lake area represents the best choice for a new recreation vehicle park development. (Data were supplied by the Webster District of the Corps of Engineers, 1972–1980.) Several important factors support the Grand Lake area in general and its south and/or west shorelines in particular:

> Grand Lake is the dominant attraction in Northwest Madison, which generates demand for groups of campers and for campers who stay four or more days.

> Within one hour's driving time there are several tourist attractions, including:

>> Ichaban Sports/Recreation Center and Oriental Restaurant on Highway 27 between Lucedale and Stevensville.

>> Hunt's Springs on Highway 60 about thirty miles northeast of Stevensville (on the eastern part of Grand Lake). This resort area is the location of an outdoor theater production that has a national reputation.

>> Big Eagle, Hickory Creek, and Bill's Creek (located on the sourth and west shorelines) are the most popular points for visitors, according to the Corps of Engineers.

>> Huntsville, the home of the University of Madison, is the area's population, employment, economic, educational, and cultural center.

> The site is accessible from both U.S. Highway 60 and U.S. Highway 78, the major thoroughfare from Bluff City to points south.

The impact of all these features is that proposed park site will have higher occupancy because camper groups will stay in the area longer. In addition, the combined drawing power of several attractions will increase repeat business year after year. Such considerations are important for the economic feasibility of destination travel-trailer parks.

A survey was undertaken for an area south and west of Grand Lake, as discussed earlier. It established the following:

1. There is a need for additional recreational-vehicle or travel-trailer spaces in the area. Past growth plus current plans for constructing a new park support this conclusion. For example, the Safari campground is currently expanding to double its capacity. Also, investors are seeking rezoning of the land on Highway 78 between Lucedale and Stevensville for an RV park development.

2. The park should contain some tent sites and no more than 100 travel-trailer spaces, based on past and projected growth in demand.

3. The market is likely to grow at the rate of 4 to 8 percent per year; therefore, future expansion is a possibility.

4. Rentals should be $7.50 per space per night, including all charges except extra occupancy—that is, more than two persons.

5. Depending on the quality of management, the park should achieve an occupancy level between 20 and 33 percent for the first year's operation, based on 360 days per year. Based on a seven-month season, the park should achieve an occupancy level between 35 and 55 percent during the first year. Aggressive marketing and management of the park should achieve the 55 percent or higher occupancy level.

The following criteria should be used in selecting a park site:

1. Locate close to a dominant recreation attraction or close to an existing destination park. Locations on the highway are more expensive, are oriented toward the overnight market, and are riskier ventures because of more intensive future competition. It would be desirable to obtain advertising/sign space on the major highway.

2. Utilities should be close at hand.

3. Terrain should be relatively flat but slightly sloping to provide water runoff. Watch out for slopes and topography that will require extensive grading.

4. Local building codes and zoning should allow a density of spaces per acre to permit profitable operation (up to ten units per acre).

5. Accessibility should include a paved road to the park site.

An analysis of the facilities offered by the competition has led to the following specifications:

1. A minimum of ten acres, preferably more.

2. A minimum of 40 spaces and a maximum of 100 spaces

3. A combination registration office and grocery store (living quarters added to the rear of the store)

4. A recreation room, a minimum of 400 square feet.

5. A laundry/restroom facility of about 625 square feet for every 30 to 35 spaces

6. A small swimming pool—20 by 40 feet

7. Crushed rock streets

8. A public pay telephone

9. Picnic tables and grills

10. A covered group shelter and picnic area

11. A playground.

Financial Analysis: Financial Feasibility

Analysis of the macro and micro demand and competition elements substantiate the market feasibility of a recreational vehicle park in the Grand Lake area (south or west side of the lake).

Attention is now directed to the financial feasibility of a park. The presentation will begin with the initial financial status and capital investment schedule. The first year's estimated income statements will be developed for four parks of different sizes: 40, 50, 60, and 100 sites. The pro forma income and expense statements for three years will be developed. Finally, investment returns and risks will be evaluated.

Certain assumptions were stated at the outset:

1. Total investment should not exceed $220,000 to $275,000.
2. Funds for equity investment are limited to $55,000.
3. Interest on mortgage or SBA loan is 11.0 percent.
4. Loan term is twenty years.
5. Land prices are $3,000 per acre.

Development Costs. In figuring the cost of land and improvements, the developer must recognize the following factors, all of which will influence the amount of investment:

Source of the water supply

Method of waste treatment

Amount of work the owner will perform

Influence of topography on grading and the like.

Taking the foregoing into consideration, Table B–22 shows development costs for four different sizes of parks with 40, 50, 60, and 100 sites, respectively. All four sizes fall within the parameters of market feasibility as analyzed in the area survey on demand and competition trends. These cost estimates are considered reasonable but are only approximate. Accurate costs cannot be identified until contractors see the specific site.

From the estimated development costs and other data collected, the proposed project's financial feasibility can be evaluated. First, an analysis of projected income and expenses for the first year will help identify the most appropriate park size—40, 50, 60, or 100 spaces. Then a five-year pro forma income projection will be made (see table B–23). The assumptions used in the table are based on analysis of income statements from the following sources: David Nulsen and Robert Nulsen, *Handbook for Developing and Operating Mobile Home and Recreational Vehicle Parks* (Beverly Hills, Calif.: Trail-R-Club of America), 1985.

Table B–22
RV Park Cost Estimates

Item	40-Site Park	50-Site Park	60-Site Park	100-Site Park	Depreciation Rate
Land[a]	$ 49,500	$ 49,500	$ 49,500	$ 49,500	0%
Basic building and recreation Room[b]	55,000	55,000	55,000	55,000	5%
Restroom and laundry[c]	8,800	13,200	13,200	17,600	5%
Tables, grills, and playgrounds	4,950	6,050	7,150	12,100	10%
Swimming and wading pools	15,400	15,400	15,400	15,400	10%
Electricity to sites[d]	6,600	7,750	8,900	13,500	10%
Water to sites[e]	5,680	6,600	7,520	11,200	5%
Sewage hookups and collection lines[f]	6,600	7,750	8,900	13,500	5%
Roads and grading[g]	10,600	11,750	12,900	17,500	5%
Supervision and miscellaneous	16,500	16,500	16,500	16,500	
Total costs	$179,630	$189,500	$194,970	$221,800	

[a]Fifteen acres at $2,750 per acre.

[b]Basic building includes registration, store, and living quarters—2,100 square feet; recreation room—400 square feet; total—2,500 square feet at $22.00 per square foot.

[c]Laundry: 10″ × 25′, two washers, two dryers, vending machines. Assume all machines are owned by others. Men's restrooms—three showers, two toilets, two urinals, three wash basins, 15′ × 12.5′; women's restrooms—three showers, four toilets, three wash basins, 15′ × 12.5′; total laundry and restrooms—625 square feet.

[d]$2,000 fixed charge plus $115,000 per space.

[e]$2,000 fixed charge plus $92,000 per space.

[f]$2,000 fixed charge plus $115,000 per space.

[g]$6,000 fixed charge plus $115,000 per space.

The bottom line in table B–23 shows net income before income taxes and debt service (mortgage payment). Note that depreciation, a noncash expense, is included as an expense. It is clear, on the basis of the stated assumptions, that either a 60-space or a 100-space park is most feasible financially. Of course, for each of the alternative sizes, the higher the occupancy level, the more profitable the operation.

For emphasis, it is important to restate the major assumption in the foregoing financial feasibility analysis: a conservative seven-month or 210-day season is used, with occupancy levels of 35 percent, 45 percent, and 55 percent. These levels translate into annual (360-day base) occupancy levels of 20, 26, and 32 percent respectively. The length of the season and the assumed occupancy levels are judged to be quite conservative in relation to the existing and expected future market potential.

Table B–24 is a five-year pro forma income projection based on a 60-space recreational vehicle park. The bottom line of table B–24 shows net operating profit (after deduction for depreciation but before income taxes and

Table B–23
Proposed Recreational-Vehicle Park Projected Income Statement by Park Size and Occupancy Level

	1	2	3
	40[d]-Site Park Occupancy Level		
	35%	45%	55%
Number of space rents[a]	2,940	3,780	4,620
Gross income	$22,050	$28,350	$34,650
Extra occupancy[b]	1,103	1,418	1,733
Vending machines[c]	1,470	1,890	2,310
Laundry[d]			
Store sales[e]	14,700	18,900	23,100
Total income[f]	39,323	50,558	61,793
Less cost of goods sold[g]	8,820	11,340	13,860
Gross profit	$30,503	$39,218	$47,933
Less Expenses			
Salaries[h]	$10,500	$10,500	$10,500
Payroll taxes[i]	1,575	1,575	1,575
Property taxes[j]	2,512	2,512	2,512
Insurance[k]	1,950	1,950	1,950
Advertising and signs	3,000	3,000	3,000
Office expense and supplies	300	300	300
Telephone[l]	600	600	600
Utilities—electric[m]	2,470	2,890	3,310
Utilities—water[n]	1,288	1,456	1,624
Maintenance—building and grounds, trash	200	200	200
Maintenance—pool	1,000	1,000	1,000
Maintenance—roads	300	300	300
Depreciation[o]	8,349	8,349	8,349
All other expenses	2,500	2,500	2,500
Total expenses	$36,544	$37,132	$37,720
Income before debt service and taxes	($6,041)	$ 2,086	$10,213

Note: Based on seven-month season (210 days).

[a]Assume a seven-month season: occupancy level 1 = 35 percent on a base of 210 days or 20 percent on 360 days; occupancy level 2 = 45 percent on a base of 210 days or 26 percent on 360 days; occupancy level 3 = 55 percent on base of 210 days or 32 percent on 360 days; space rents = $7.50 per night.

[b]Extra occupancy. Assume 5 percent of space income (this is low, since average party size is 2.9 persons).

[c]$0.25/space/night.

[d]$0.25/space/night/net (no investment).

[e]$5.00/space night.

[f]Total income does not include possible tent site rentals.

debt service) rising from $18,654 in 1987 to nearly $42,000 in 1991—an increase of 123 percent over the five-year period. These projections are based on aggressive management and marketing practices and on management's willingness to offer a competitive total amenity package. Occupancy levels will increase through repeat business only if campers find a number of recreational alternatives that meet their needs.

4	5	6	7	8	9	10	11	12
50-Site Park Occupancy Level			60-Site Park Occupancy Level			100 Park Sites Occupancy Level		
35%	45%	55%	35%	45%	55%	35%	45%	55%
3,675	4,725	5,775	4,410	5,670	6,930	7,350	9,450	11,500
$27,563	$35,438	$43,313	$33,075	$42,525	$51,975	$55,125	$ 70,875	$ 86,625
1,378	1,772	2,166	1,654	2,126	2,599	2,756	3,544	4,331
1,838	2,363	2,888	2,205	2,835	3,465	3,675	4,725	5,775
18,375	23,625	28,875	22,050	28,350	34,350	36,750	47,250	57,750
49,154	63,198	77,242	58,984	75,836	92,689	98,306	126,394	154,481
11,025	14,175	17,325	13,230	17,010	20,790	22,050	28,350	34,650
$38,129	$49,023	$59,917	$45,754	$58,826	$71,899	$76,256	$ 98,044	$119,831
$10,500	$10,500	$10,500	$10,500	$10,500	$10,500	$15,750	$ 15,750	$ 15,750
1,575	1,575	1,575	1,575	1,575	1,575	2,363	2,363	2,363
2,723	2,723	2,723	2,723	2,723	2,723	4,200	4,200	4,200
2,160	2,160	2,160	2,160	2,160	2,160	3,225	3,225	3,225
3,000	3,000	3,000	3,000	3,000	3,000	3,000	3,000	3,000
300	300	300	300	300	300	300	300	300
600	600	600	600	600	600	600	600	600
2,838	3,363	3,888	3,205	3,835	4,465	4,675	5,725	6,775
1,435	1,645	1,855	1,582	1,834	2,086	2,170	2,590	3,010
200	200	200	200	200	200	200	200	200
1,000	1,000	1,000	1,000	1,000	1,000	1,000	1,000	1,000
300	300	300	300	300	300	300	300	300
8,899	8,899	8,899	9,226	9,226	9,226	10,815	10,815	10,815
2,500	2,500	2,500	2,500	2,500	2,500	2,500	2,500	2,500
$38,030	$38,765	$39,500	$39,290	$40,172	$41,054	$51,098	$ 52,568	$ 54,038
$ 99	$10,258	$20,417	$ 6,464	$18,654	$30,845	$25,158	$ 45,476	$ 65,793

[g]CGS = 60 percent; 40 percent markup on retail.
[h]Salaries = $1,500 per month (two men at $750/month for seven months).
[i]Payroll taxes = 15 percent of payroll.
[j]Property taxes = 1.5 percent of $200,000 property value.
[k]Insurance = 1.5 percent of building.
[l]Telephone = $50.00 per month for business and listing.
[m]Electricity = $1,000 + $.50/camper night.
[n]Water = $700 + $0.20/camper night.
[o]Straight line depreciation based on depreciation rates in the table.

The investment analysis shows that a total investment of $183,000 will require $55,000 in equity, since it will be difficult to secure a mortgage loan in principal amount for more than a 70 percent loan-to-value ratio ($128,000).

The ROI calculations show a first-year return of 18.9 percent (net cash flow in the first year of $10,431 divided by equity of $55,000) (see table B–25). Though not spectacular, this is definitely acceptable for the first year's operation.

Table B–24
Sixty-Space Recreational-Vehicle Park Pro Forma Income Projections

	1987	1988	1989	1990	1991
Number of space rents[a]	5,670	5,922	6,174	6,552	6,930
Gross income	$42,525	$46,665	$51,587	$ 57,976	$ 64,465
Extra occupancy	2,126	2,333	2,579	2,899	3,223
Vending machines and laundry	2,835	2,961	3,087	3,276	3,465
Store sales[b]	28,350	31,185	34,304	37,734	41,507
Total income	$75,836	$83,144	$91,557	$101,885	$112,660
Less cost of goods sold	17,010	18,711	20,582	22,640	24,904
Gross profit	$58,826	$64,433	$79,975	$ 79,245	$ 87,756
Less expenses[c]					
Salaries	$10,500	$11,200	$11,800	$ 12,500	$ 13,250
Payroll taxes	1,575	1,670	1,770	1,875	2,000
Property taxes	2,932	2,932	2,932	2,932	2,932
Insurance	2,370	2,500	2,500	2,650	2,650
Advertising and signs	3,000	3,200	3,500	3,900	4,000
Office expense—supplies	300	320	350	380	420
Telephone	600	600	660	725	800
Utilities—electric	3,835	3,961	4,087	4,276	4,465
Utilities—water	1,834	1,884	1,934	2,010	2,086
Maintenance—building and grounds	200	200	210	210	210
Maintenance—pool	1,000	1,060	1,125	1,200	1,275
Maintenance—roads	300	300	320	320	320
Depreciation	9,226	9,226	9,226	9,226	9,226
All other	2,500	2,500	2,500	2,500	2,500
Total expenses	40,172	41,553	42,914	44,704	46,134
Net operating income before taxes and debt service	$18,654	$22,880	$28,061	$34,541	$41,622

[a]Rents will grow at a rate of about 6.0 percent per year. Through better management and market growth, occupancy level will increase 2.0 percent per year in 1988 and 1989 and 3.0 percent per year in 1990 and 1991.
[b]Store sales will increase 10.0 percent per year.
[c]Selected expenses will increase 6.0 to 10.0 percent per year.

Aggressive management will be required to (1) increase rental rates by 6 percent a year, (2) increase occupancy levels by 2 to 3 percent a year, and (3) hold increases in expenses down to 6 percent a year. Under these conditions the ROI increases to a desirable 38.7 percent (net cash flow in the fifth year of $26,099 divided by equity of $67,400) (see table B–25).

During the first full year of operation, the sum of salaries and net cash flow is more than $20,000. This amount does not include "free" rent on living quarters. By the end of the fifth year, the sum of payroll and net cash flow has risen to a healthy $41,349. Factoring in a 6 percent annual rate of inflation, the $41,349 is equal to $30,000 in today's purchasing power.

Table B–25
Return on Investment Calculations

	First Year	Fifth Year
A. Income tax schedule		
1. Net operating income	$18,654	$41,622
2. Deduct interest on mortgage[a]	14,080	12,716
3. Income subject to tax	4,574	28,906
4. Tax (assume 3 percent)	.3	.3
5. Income taxes	1,372	8,672
B. Cash flow schedule		
1. Net operating income	18,654	41,622
2. Add back depreciation	9,226	9,226
3. Balance	27,880	50,848
4. Deduct mortgage payment	16,077	16,077
5. Deduct income taxes	1,372	8,672
6. Net cash flow	10,431	26,099
C. Return on investment		
1. Initial inestment	55,000	55,000
2. Add equity buildup from mortgage	0	12,400
3. Total investment	55,000	55,000
4. Return on investment—net cash flow, total	18.9%	38.7%

[a]11.0 percent interest rate, original principal of $128,000, paid down to $115,600 at the end of the fifth year.

Analysis of Existing Park for Sale

Two RV parks are for sale in the Grand Lake area: the Yogi Bear Jellystone Park (60 units for $650,000) and Jim Bob's Trailer Park (39 units for $165,000). Price eliminates Jellystone from consideration. The following is an analysis of the Jim Bob property.

A 39-space combination mobile-recreational vehicle park is on the market in the Hickory Creek area. The asking price is $165,000. Following is an evaluation of this park as an alternative to developing a new park:

1. Owner's income statement
2. Price and cost analysis
3. Reconstructed income statement
4. ROI analysis

Owner's income statement (unaudited, available from real estate broker) income and expense date annualized from a six-month statement for the period ending June 30, 1978).

Income:

Space rents (25)	$ 8,142	
Mobile home rental	10,388	
Miscellaneous	180	
Total income		$18,710
Less Expenses		
Utilities	$ 6,332	
Auto expense	1,242	
Office supplies	234	
Laundry	82	
Travel	106	
Maintenance	2,064	
Unit supplies	664	
Advertising	1,142	
Taxes	1,598	
Other	32	
Total expenses		$13,496
Net operating income		$ 5,214

An evaluation of Jim Bob's Trailer Park includes the following: RV space rents for $4.00 per night. Based on a 210-day season (seven months), the $8,142 reported represents a 25 percent occupancy level. Such a low performance can be attributed to a low-amenity, low-price marketing strategy. Since the overall market demand in the Hickory Creek area is strong and increasing (based on Madison Corps of Engineers studies in 1977 and 1982), this strategy does not reach the market of those who want more amenities and are willing to pay for them. Therefore, any consideration of this existing park should be from the standpoint of adding sufficient quality and quantity of amenities to increase market penetration and hence the occupancy level.

The second income item, mobile-home rentals, provides a stabilizing and positive element in this investment opportunity. The $10,388 breaks down exactly. Nevertheless, the year-round nature of this source of income has some definite advantages.

A review of the expenses shows them to be lacking in salaries, insurance, and advertising (which is low). Telephone utilities seem to be quite high and should be examined. The following is a reconstructed income statement reflecting an increase in investment (amenities).

2. *Price and cost analysis.* Jim Bob's Trailer Park is offered for sale for $165,000. Using a gross capitalization rate in the range of 13 to 15 percent, a counteroffer in the range of $125,000–$145,000 is appropriate. Assume the

high end of the value range—$145,000. The following amenities need to be constructed.

Recreation room and store (1,000 square feet)	$ 20,000
Restroom and laundry	8,000
Tables, grills, and playground	4,500
Swimming and wading pools	14,000
Total additional investment	$ 46,500
Purchase price (estimated)	145,000
	$191,500

3. *Reconstructed first-year income statement*

Income:

Space rents (45 percent occupancy @ $7.50)	$ 27,638
MH pad rentals (10 pads @ 70 percent occupancy)	7,140
MH units rentals (3 units @ $200.00)	7,200
Store sales—RV campers	14,700
Store sales—MH units ($50/month)	6,000
Total income	$ 62,678
Less cost of goods sold	12,420
Gross profit	$ 50,258
Less expenses	35,805
Net operating profit	$ 14,453

4. *ROI Analysis*

Net operating profit	$ 14,453
Add back depreciation	7,610
Subtotal	22,063
Less income taxes (30 percent tax bracket)	0
Less debt service (11.0 percent, 20 year mortgage)	17,772
Net cash flow	$ 4,291

Using similar economic and financial data as shown in table B–25, this alternative of purchasing an existing RV park produces greater net cash flow than purchasing the comparable newly constructed park ($2,086 for 40 units, 45 percent occupancy level). More favorable seller financing for part of the purchased park would also increae ROI. Of course, additional land is available for development. Increasing the number of RV spaces to 50 or 60 will greatly increase the profitability of this investment opportunity.

The foregoing has been presented to give the reader an idea of how to analyze the purchase alternative. A scheme involving different amenities or added spaces might prove to be more financially feasible should investment funds be tight.

Internal Analysis: How to File an Application
for an SBA Loan under the Guaranty Plan

How Does the Guaranty Plan Work? The Guaranty Plan makes it possible for you to file an application for a loan directly with your bank at a reasonable interest rate, providing the following facts exist and the use of proceeds is for eligible purposes:

1. That your relationship and credit standing is good with your bank.

2. That the loan applied for can be secured with collateral that you own now or that is to be purchased from the proceeds of the loan and that is considered by the bank to be adequate to reasonably secure the loan.

3. That the balance sheet shows the net worth of your existing business or the new business to be established to be approximately equal to the amount of the loan requested, and that the ratio of indebtedness to net worth is not considered excessive.

4. That the past operating statements of your existing business show the ability to retire the loan from earnings or, in the case of a new business, that a three-year projection of earnings will show necessary profits to retire the loan.

5. That your past records of handling obligations with the bank and other business firms with which you are dealing is satisfactory.

6. That you and any officers of your corporation have not been adjudicated a bankrupt, or connected with a receivership, or involved in any criminal or subversive activities or in other legal proceedings of a detrimental nature.

7. That, if you have an existing business, you can provide a balance sheet not over ninety days old and operating statements for the past three years. If it is a business to be purchased, we will need the reason for selling, copies of income tax returns on the business for the past three years, and a personal balance sheet over ninety days old on you as the applicant. If it is a new business to be established, we will need a pro forma balance sheet on the business and a three-year projection of earnings.

With the foregoing information, we would like an opportunity to assist you in presenting your application to your bank of account in good form. There is no charge for our services.

What Is Meant by a Long-Term Commitment?. If the collateral offered to secure the loan is long lasting, such as land and buildings, a maximum period of fifteen years can be considered on new construction and ten years on existing building.

If the loan is for working capital, inventory, machinery, equipment, or the like, the term generally will be five years, with a maximum of six years.

Further Information. The most valuable asset a borrower can have is good established bank credit. Any supplier seeking credit information contacts your bank. SBA helps you establish this credit. The majority of the banks in the country are familiar with the Guaranty Plan. If your application has merit and is considered feasible, the bank will usually consider submitting your application to its discount committee, once it is properly prepared.

We will process your application within approximately fifteen days after it is received, depending on our backlog at the time.

Minimum bank participation is 10 percent or the amount of present indebtedness to the bank, whichever is greater.

Procedure

1. Assemble the information outlined herein.
2. Take it to your bank and ask your banker to review the information and loan proposal. (As we have no direct funds, it will be necessary for you to locate a bank that is willing to participate with SBA and make the loan.)
3. If the bank is willing to participate, ask the bank to forward the information to us for our review, along with their comments.

Information Needed for Loan Review

1. Brief resume of business.
2. Brief resume of management setting forth prior business experience, technical training, education, age, health, and so on.
3. Itemized use of loan proceeds:

Working capital	$_____
Land	$_____
Building	$_____
Furniture and fixtures	$_____
Machinery and equipment	$_____
Automotive equipment	$_____
Other	$_____
Total	$_____

4. Current business balance sheet and profit/loss statement
5. Year-end business balance sheets and profit/loss statements for the last three years or, if the business has been in existence less than three years, financial statements for each year it has been in operation. (Copies of the financial statements submitted with income tax returns are adequate.)

6. If the business is not in existence but is proposed, furnish a projected balance sheet of the business showing its proposed assets, liabilities, and net worth upon commencement of operations, together with projected annual operating statements for the first two years of operation.

7. Furnish a separate personal balance sheet showing all assets owned and liabilities owed outside of the business.

The foregoing is the information a loan officer will need to properly analyze your loan proposal.

Index

Abell, D.F., 24 *n*.2
Absolute market potential, 32, 33–34
Absolute market share, 23
Acceptance rate, 35, 59–61; method of estimating sales, 130
Account, key, 31
Activity ratio of asset turnover, 80
Advantages, differential, 42–43, 51
Agricultural Statistics, 65
Alderson, S., 53 *n*.5
Almanac of Business and Industrial Financial Ratios, 111
Alternatives: determining most beneficial, 82; identification of, 81; sample analysis of; 173–175
American Statistics Index: A Comprehensive Guide and Index to the Statistical Publications of the U.S. Government, 107
Annual Survey of Manufacturers, 112
Ansoff, H.I., 20
Arbitrary judgment. *See* Judgment estimates
Arizona Public Service Company, corporate objectives of, 17–19
Audit, competitive market mix, 47–49
Average return on investment, 84
Ayer Directory of Publications, 107

Backward integration, 21
Bank credit, 177
Barriers, entry, 45
Behavior: consumer, 31; cost, 66–74
Benefit segmentation, 28
Benefit/cost analysis for nonprofit entity, 92

Benefit/cost ratio of discounted cash flows, 88–89
Blaho, Inc., sample opportunity analysis report for, 117–135
Boston Consulting Group, 22
Breakdown approach to market segmentation, 29–30
Break-even analysis, sensitivity analysis as illustrated by, 66–70
Break-even point, 67–69
Building costs, sample analysis of, 144–146, 154
Buildup approach to market segmentation, 30–31
Bulova Co., 99
Bureau of the Census Catalog, 107
Business Conditions Digest, 107
Business Cycle Developments, 107
Business Periodicals Index, 66, 107
Business Publication Rates and Data, 112
Business Statistics, 107
Buyer. *See* Consumer

Capabilities, matching market opportunities to organizational, 12–14
Capital budgeting: decision flow chart for, 80–82; for equipment, 73; methods of analyzing investments, 82–93; sensitivity analysis in, 70. *See also* Cost analysis: Financial analysis; Profitability analysis
Cash cows, 23, 24
Cash flow: concept, economic, 82; discounted, benefit/cost ratio of, 88–89; discounted, present value of, 85–86; risk-adjusted, 90–91

Census reports: *Census of Business,* 107; *Census of Housing,* 107; *Census of Manufacturers,* 107–108, 112; *Census of Retail Trade,* 108; *Census of Selected Service Industries,* 108; *Census of the Population,* 110; *Census of Transportation,* 108; *Census of Wholesale Trade,* 108; cost data from, 65
Chakmas, P.C., 53 *n.*3
Challengers, market, 51–52
Colowyo Coal Company, 15
Committed fixed costs, 63
Commodity Yearbook, 108
Comparative pricing, 49, 50
Competition as external factor in market opportunity analysis, 6
Competitive analysis, 39–55; competitive advantages, 42–43, 51; data sources for, 111–112; environment, effects of, 40–42; industry analysis in, 43–46; level of competition and, 41; market mix audit, 47–49; nature of competition and, 41–42; positioning company/product in, 51–52; purpose of, 39; in sample reports, 127–129, 160–163; specific competitor analysis in, 46–47; of strategies and resources, 49–51; types of competition, 40–41, 42, 51, 128–129
Competitive approaches, evaluating different, 47
Computer simulation, 91
Conglomerate diversification, 21–22, 100
Consumer: acceptance of technology, 7, 125; characteristics and needs of potential, 29–31, 124–125; classifications of, 28; composition, industry analysis of, 44; data sources on, 110–111; demand, sample analysis of, 140–141; identification of potential, 164; surveys, 35, 36–37, 59–61
Consumer market and Magazine Report, 110
Controllable costs, 63–64
Corporate objectives, 8, 13, 16–19
Corporate purpose, 13
Correlation analysis, 32

Cost analysis, 57, 58, 61–77; cost behavior and, 66–74; cost concepts, 61–62; data sources on, 65–66, 112–113; estimates, 7, 8, 71–72; forecast checklist, 71; forecasting procedures, 74–77; for nonprofit entities, 91–93; risk analysis and, 70–71; in sample reports, 131–132, 142–151, 154, 168–175; sensitivity analysis and, 66–70; technical analysis, 72–74
Cost-effectiveness analysis, 92–93
Costs: change over product's life cycle, 57; overhead, 4; in profitability analysis, identification of relevant, 81–82; types of, 62–64, 67–69, 75
County and City Data Book, 108
County Business Patterns, 108
Credit, bank, 177
Crest Report (Chain Restaurant Eating Out Share Trends), 110

Data, sources of, 31, 107–113; competitive, 111–112; consumer, 110–111; cost, 65–66, 112–113; industry/market, 107–110
Decision flow chart for profitability analysis, 80–82
Decision making. *See* Strategic planning
Delphi technique, 35
Demand analysis. *See* Market demand analysis
Demographic segmentation, 28
Department of Commerce, 66
"Designer" approach to operating organization, 4
Development: costs, sample analysis of, 168–173; market, 21; product, 20–21
Dialogue, organizational, 12
Differential advantages, 42–43, 51
Differential costs, 64
Direct costs, 63
Directories of Federal Statistics for Local Areas and for States: Guides to Sources, 108
Directory of Corporate Affiliations, 111
Directory of Intercorporate Ownership, 111

Discount rate, risk-adjusted, 89–90
Discounted cash flow: benefit/cost ratio of, 88–89; method of making capital budgeting decisions, 70; present value of, 85–86
Discretionary fixed costs, 63
Diversification strategies, 21–22, 100
Dogs, strategic business units classified as, 23, 24
Dow Jones Industrial average, 3
Drilling industry, sample analysis of, 121–123
Drucker, P.F., 14, 16

Economic Almanac, 108
Economic cash flow concept, 82
Economic Census, 112
Economic Indicators, 108
Economy: as external factor in market opportunity analysis, 6; within industry, analysis of, 45–46; sample analysis of, 159–160. *See also* Competitive analysis
Eisenhower, D.D., 12
Employee expenses, sample analysis of, 149–150, 151
Encyclopedia of Association, 112
Entry, ease of: barriers, 45; competition type and, 40–41; effect of competitive environment on, 42; sample analysis of, 128–129
Environment: competitive, 40–42; natural, 7; political risk in, 6–7; sample analysis of, 120–121. *See also* Competitive analysis; Market demand analysis
Equipment costs, 73, 146
Exit, ease of, 42
Expansion strategies, 19–22
Expenses, sample analysis of operating, 148–151. *See also* Cost analysis
Experiments, cost data from, 65
External analysis in sample reports, 119–123, 140–143, 158–160. *See also* Competitive analysis; Market demand analysis
External factors in market opportunity analysis, 6–7, 13
Facility costs, sample analysis of, 143–147
Federal Reserve Bulletin, 108–109

Financial analysis: defined, 80; forecasting market share, 59–61; nonprofit, 58–59; profitability analysis, 79–93; in sample reports, 129–135, 142–153, 168–175. *See also* Cost analysis
Financial factors in market opportunity analysis, 7–8
Financial resources, 50, 100, 101, 102
Finished goods inventory, 72
Fixed costs, 62–63, 67, 68, 69
Fixed investment, 75
Followers, market, 47, 52
Food Service Trends, 110
Forecasting: of costs, 71–72, 74–77; market share, 59–61; sales, samples of, 129–132; three-level method of, 12, 90
Fortune Directory, 111
Fortune Double 500 Directory, 111
Forward integration, 21
Frank, N., 109

General Motors, 6
Geographic segmentation, 28
Government regulations, 6
Grids, market, 29–31
Growth strategies, basic, 19–22
Guaranty plan, SBA loan under, 176–178
Guide to Consumer Markets, 111
Guppy strategy, 52

Halo effect, 49
Handbook for Developing and Operating Mobile Home and Recreational Vehicle Parks (Nulsen & Nulsen), 168
Handbook of Economic Statistics, 109
Hedley, B., 22
Historical cost data, 65, 76
Historical perspective, sample report giving, 120
Historical Statistics of the U.S. from Colonial Times to 1957, 111
Horizontal integration, 21

Identification: of alternatives, 81; of market, 27–31; of market opportunities, 19–24
Incremental cost, 64
Indirect costs, 63

Industry analysis, 43–46; common issues and problems, 46; data sources for, 107–110; for driving mechanisms, 44–45, 46; evaluation factors, 45; sample reports giving, 120, 121–123, 158–159; for structure and direction, 44
Inflation, 6
Integrative strategies, 21
Interdependent strategic maneuvers, industry analysis of, 44
Internal analysis: differentiation of problems and opportunities in, 97–98; of financial resources, 100, 101, 102; of managerial resources, 100–101, 102; of marketing resources, 98–99, 101, 102; of physical resources, 99, 101, 102; of purpose, 98; ranking opportunities, 101–103; in sample reports, 133–134, 176–178; of strengths and weaknesses, 101, 102; worksheet, 103
Internal factors in market opportunity analysis, 8
Internal rate of return (IRR), 87–88
Interviews, cost data from, 65
Inventory: estimates, 72–73; types of 72
Investment: fixed, 75; methods of analyzing, 82–93; political risk of overseas, 7; return on, 8, 57, 79–80, 84, 132, 153; sample analysis of, 171–172, 173; turnover activity ratio of, 80
IRR, 87–88

Japanese, emphasis on market share by, 3–4
Judgment estimates, 32; of market share, 59; to forecast costs, 76; of market potential, 35

Key account, 31
Kotler, P., 24 *n*.1, 53 *n*.6

Labor requirements and costs, estimating, 73–74
Land costs, sample analysis of, 143–144
Leaders, market, 47, 51
Legislation, government, 6

Level of competition, 41
Loan, SBA, 176–178
Location analysis, sample of, 165–167

Management: differential advantages in, 43; level, controlled vs. uncontrollable costs by, 64; resources in, 100–101, 102; strategic, process of, 12–14
Manufacturing costs, 75
Manville Corporation, 3
Marginal costs, 64
Market: data sources on, 107–110; development, 21; expansion strategies, 20–21; grids, 29–31; growth matrix, 19, 20; identification of, 27–31; penetration, 20, 59–61; -related diversification, 21; target, 164. *See also* Segmentation, market
Market Analysis: A Handbook of Current Data Sources (Frank), 109
Market demand analysis, 27–37; estimating potential, 32–37; identifying a market, 27–31; market factors in, 31–37; in sample reports, 121–123, 140–141, 158–160
Market factor method of estimating market potential, 33–34
Market Guide, 109
Market mix audit, competitive, 47–49
Market opportunity analysis: defined, 8–9; factors influencing, 5–8, 9; importance of, 3
Market potential, 32–37; absolute vs. relative, 32–34; defined, 32, 141; estimating, for existing products, 32–34, 35; estimating, for new products or services, 34–37; sample analysis of, 118, 126–127, 140–143
Market share: forecasting, 59–61; Japanese emphasis on, 3–4; relative vs. absolute, 23
Marketing: differential advantages in, 43; mix, 164; resources, 98–99, 101, 102; resources, assessing competitor's, 50; strategy, sample analysis of, 160–161, 163–165
Marketing Information Guide, 111
McGregor, C.H., 53 *n*.3

Measuring Markets: A Guide to the Use of Federal and State Statistical Data, 109
Merchandising (magazine), 109
Middle Market Directory, 111
Milk cows strategy, 24
Million Dollar Directory, 111
Mission, corporate, 8, 13, 14–15
MKT, 7
Monopolistic competition, 40, 42
Monopoly, 41, 42
Monthly Labor Review, 109
Moody's Industrial Manual, 111
Moody's Investors Services, Inc., 113
Moody's Manual of Investments, 111
Moody's Manuals, 111
Multiple regression analysis: estimating market potential using, 35; to forecast costs, 77

Natural monopoly, 41
Natural resources, differential advantages in, 43
Nature as external factor in market opportunity analysis, 7
Net-present-value (NPV) method, 85–86; relation to internal rate of return, 87; sensitivity analysis of, 89
New businesses, sample reports for, 137–178; for manufacturing business, 137–154; for service business, 155–178
New products and services, estimating market potential for, 34–37
Nichers, market, 47, 52
Noncontrollable costs, 63–64
Nonprofit entities: cost analysis for, 91–93; financial analysis of, 58–59
Nulsen, D., 168
Nulsen, R., 168
Number of firms, effect of competitive environment on, 42

Objectives, corporate, 8, 13, 16–19
Oil and Gas Journal, 127
Oil crisis of 1974, 6
Oligopolistic competition, 40–41, 42, 51, 128–129
Operating expenses, sample analysis of, 148–151

Opportunities, market: aligning organizational resources with, 97–104; defined, 97; identifying, 19–24; problems vs., 97–98; ranking, 101–103
Opportunity costs, 64
Organization: capabilities, matching market opportunities to, 12–14; positioning of, 51–52; statement of purpose or mission, 8. *See also* Resources, organizational
Organizational dialogue, 12
Original equipment manufacturers as potential customer, 124–125, 126, 128
Overhead costs, 4
Overseas investment, political risk in, 7

PAIS, 109
Payback period, 83–84
Penetration, market, 20; forecasting rate of, 59–61
Percentage-of-sales method to forecast costs, 77
Period costs, 62
Pfizer, Inc., Leeming/Pacquin Division of, 50
Philip Morris, Inc., 5
Physical resources, 99, 101, 102
Pillsbury Company, financial goals and objectives of, 16–17
Pilot plant or process activities, cost data from, 65
Place: effect of competitive environment on, 42; sample analysis of, 164–167
Planning: plans as distinct from, 12; short-term, 3–4. *See also* Strategic planning
Political conditions as external factor in market opportunity analysis, 6–7
Porter, M.E., 53*n*.2
Positioning of company/product, 50, 51–52
Potential consumers, characteristics of, 29–31, 124–125
Potential, market. *See* Market potential
Predicasts, 109
Present value method of analyzing investments, 85–86; in sample reports, 152
Present-value index, 88–89

Price: comparative pricing, 49, 50; effect of competitive environment on, 42; sample analysis of, 165, 174–175; sensitivity analysis of profits and, 69, 70

Pro forma income statement, 74; defined, 57; developing, 58; in sample reports, 129–132, 151–152, 153, 168, 170–171, 172

Proactive strategies, 50

Probability distributions of expected returns, 89, 90

Problem: definition, 81; opportunities vs., 97–98

Problem children, strategic business units classified as, 23, 24

Product: acceptance rate of, 35, 59–61, 130; costs, 62; development, 20–21; effect of competitive environment on, 42; estimating potential for existing, 32–34, 35; estimating potential for new, 34–37; expansion strategies, 20–21; growth matrix, 19, 20; life cycle, revenue and cost changes over, 57; positioning, 50, 51–52; -related diversification, 21; substitutes, availability of good, 45; use, segmentation by, 28

Production: assessing competitor's resources in, 50; capacity, 99, 118, 132–133; differential advantages in, 43; schedule, 73; sensitivity analysis of profits and, 69, 70; space estimates for, 74; variable costs of, 63, 118

Profit margin on sales, 80

Profitability analysis, 79–93; costs analysis for nonprofit entities, 91–93; decision flow chart for, 80–82; internal rate of return, 87–88; methods of analyzing investment, 82–93; net-present-value, 85–86, 87, 89; payback period, 83–84; present-value index, 88–89; return on investment, 8, 57, 79–80, 84, 132, 153; risk analysis, 70–71, 89–91; simulation models for, 91; time value methods of, 84–89

Profits, sensitivity analysis of, 69, 70

Project cost summary, 74, 75

Promotion, 42, 165

Psychological characteristics of consumers, 31

Pure competition, 40, 42

Purpose, corporate, 8, 13; alignment between market activities and, 98; defined, 14; as reference point for action, 14–15

Quantified objectives, 16

Rand McNally Commercial Atlas and Marketing Guide, 109

Ranking opportunities, 101–103

Raw materials, 72, 142–143

Reactive strategies, 49–50

Reader's Guide to Periodical Literature, 109

Reference Book of Corporate Managements, 112

Regression analysis method of estimating market potential, 34, 35

Regulations, government, 6

Relative market potential, 32; sales index measure of, 33

Relative market share, 23

Replacement potential, 35–36; sample analysis of, 124–125, 126, 128

Reports, sample, 115–178; for diversified company in petroleum industry, 117–135; for new business in manufacturing, 137–154; for new service business, 155–178

Research and development, differential advantages in, 43. *See also* Technology

Resistance to strategic planning, 11–12

Resources, organizational, 8; aligning market opportunities with, 97–104; analysis of, 98–101, 102; competitive, 49, 50–51; financial, 50, 100, 101, 102; managerial, 100–101, 102; marketing, 50, 98–99, 101, 102; natural, differential advantages in, 43; physical, 50, 99, 101, 102

Return on investment (ROI), 8, 57, 132; average, 84; calculating, 79–80; defined, 79; sample analysis of, 118, 153, 171–172, 173; simple, 84

Returns, probability distributions of expected, 89, 90

Revenue analysis, 57, 58; estimates, 7; forecasting market share, 59–61; identification of relevant revenues, 81–82; in sample reports, 131, 147–148. *See also* Cost analysis; Sales

Revenues, change over product's life cycle, 57

Rewaldt, S.H., *53n.4*, 101

Risk, political, 6–7

Risk analysis, 70–71, 89–91; risk-adjusted cash flow, 90–91; risk-adjusted discount rate, 89–90

ROI. *See* Return on investment (ROI)

Rollco Packing Company, sample opportunity analysis report for, 137–154

Sales: acceptance rate method of estimating, 130; expansion of, 20–21; forecast, samples of, 129–132; profit margin on, 80. *See also* Revenue analysis

Sales index measure of relative potential, 33

Sales Management Survey of Buying Power, 109

Sample reports, 115–178; cost analyses in, 131–132, 142–151, 154, 168–175; for diversified company in petroleum industry, 117–135; external analyses in, 119–123, 140–143, 158–160; financial analyses in, 129–135, 142–153, 168–175; internal analyses in, 133–134, 176–178; for new business in manufacturing, 137–154; for new service business, 155–178

SBA loan under guaranty plan, 176–178

SBU. *See* Strategic business unit (SBU)

Scatter diagram, 76, 77

Schedule, production, 73

Scott, J.R., *53n.4*, 101

Segmentation, market, 27–31; bases for, 28; breakdown approach to, 29–30; buildup approach to, 30–31; rationale for, 27; in sample reports, 124–125, 128

Semivariable costs, 63

Sensitivity analysis, 66–70, 89

Services: estimating potential for new, 34–37; sample opportunity report for new business in, 155–178

Sheldon's Retail Directory of the United States and Canada, 112

Shine stars strategy, 24

Shoot dogs strategy, 24

Short-term planning, 3–4

Simple return on investment, 84

Simulation models for analyzing investments, 91

Site analysis, sample of, 165–167

Size of market, 6; segmentation by, 125

Social change as external factor in market opportunity analysis, 7

Socioeconomic characteristics of consumers, 31

Solve problems strategy, 24

Southwest Airlines, 100

Space requirements and costs, estimating, 74

Special Tabulations, 113

Standard & Poor's, 65

Standard & Poor's Industry Surveys, 65, 109

Standard & Poor's Register of Corporations, Directors and Executives, 112

Standard & Poor's Trade and Securities Statistics, 110

Standard Corporation Records, 113

Stars, strategic business units classified as, 23, 24

Start-up costs, 75

State Manufacturing Directories, 112

Statistical Abstract of the United States, 110

Statistics of Income, 110

Stevens, R.E., 103

Strategic business unit (SBU), 13–14; classifications of, 23; criteria met by, 14; positioning, 51; strategies for existing, 22–24

Strategic fit, 11

Strategic planning: as key to success, 4–5; reasons for, 3–4; resistance to, 11–12; process, 12–14

Strategies, corporate, 19–24; basic growth, 19–22; competitive, 49–50; definitions of, 5; development process of, 5; diversification,

Strategies: (*Continued*)
21–22; for existing strategic
business units, 22–24; integrative,
21; product/market expansion,
20–21
Strengths, analysis of, 101, 102
Strickland, A.J., 52*n*.1
Structure, industry, 44
Substitute method of estimating market
potential, 35–36
Sunk costs, 64
Supplier composition, analysis of, 44–
45
Supplies, sample analysis of availabil-
ity of, 141–142
Survey of Buying Power, 66, 110
Survey of Current Business, 110
Surveys: consumer, 35, 36–37, 59–61;
to forecast costs, 76

Tactical decisions, basis in strategy
of, 5
Target market, 164
Technical cost analysis, 72–74
Technological agility, 99
Technology: consumer acceptance of,
7, 125; differential advantages in,
43; as external factor in market op-
portunity analysis, 6; -related diver-
sification, 21
Thomas Register, 66
Thompson, A.A., 52*n*.1
Three-level method of forecasting, 12,
90

Time intervals, period costs according
to, 62
Time studies, cost data from, 65
Time value methods of analyzing investments, 85–89
Tourism and recreation industry, sample analysis of, 158–159
Trade publications, cost data from,
65
Travel-trailer park, sample analysis
report for, 155–178
Trend analysis to forecast costs,
76–77
Turnover activity ratio of investment,
80

U.S. Industrial Outlook, 110
Urethane impellers, sample analysis
report for, 117–135

Variable costs, 63; in break-even analysis, 67, 68, 69

W.T. Grant, 100
Wall Street Journal Index, 112
Warshaw, M.R., 53*n*.4, 101
Weaknesses, analysis of, 101, 102
"What if" analysis, 66–70
Wholesale Prices and Price Indexes,
65
Working capital requirements, sample
analysis of, 146–147
Work-in-process inventory, 72
Worksheet, opportunity analysis, 103

About the Authors

Robert E. Stevens is professor of marketing in the College of Business Administration at Northeast Louisiana University in Monroe, Louisiana. Dr. Stevens's business experience includes four years of field work for a manufacturer, management of a family business, and work as a consultant for a Tulsa-based research organization. His research and writing activities have involved financial markets, oil industry reports, feasibility studies, and custom research projects. Dr. Stevens holds a B.S. in business from Arkansas State University and an M.B.A. and Ph.D. from the University of Arkansas, where he majored in marketing. Dr. Stevens has done research and consulting work for a variety of firms at both the local and national levels. He is the author of four books and more than thirty articles published in business periodicals, including *Study Guide to Contemporary Marketing, Strategic Marketing Plan Master Guide, How to Prepare a Feasibility Study,* and *The Marketing Research Handbook.*

Philip K. Sherwood is director of research at Winona Research in Minneapolis, Minnesota. Dr. Sherwood's professional interests are in the areas of marketing research, strategic planning, and feasibility analysis. His background includes consulting projects in the financial, health care, media, computer, and energy sectors. For over three years Dr. Sherwood was executive vice-president of a Tulsa-based marketing research firm. Prior to that he was a business professor at a local university and program director of the Indiana Memorial Union. He holds a B.A. in political science, an M.B.A. from the University of Hawaii, and a doctorate in administration from Indiana University. He has written numerous articles as well as two chapters of a popular management text. He is co-author of *How to Prepare a Feasibility Study* and *The Marketing Research Handbook,* both published by Prentice-Hall.